# The Idea
## of a
# Christian College

by
**Arthur F. Holmes**

**WILLIAM B. EERDMANS PUBLISHING CO.** • **Grand Rapids**

**Library of Congress Cataloging in Publication Data**

Holmes, Arthur Frank, 1924-
  The idea of a Christian college.

  Bibliography: p. 117
  1. Church and college.   I. Title.
LC383.H57        377′.8        74-19177
ISBN 0-8028-1592-8

*Reprinted, October 1975*

*To Joy and Don*
*who share these ideals*

# CONTENTS

# PREFACE

Over the last ten years I have been privileged to give addresses, lectures and papers on various aspects of Christian higher education at a number of Christian colleges and organizations across the United States. Some have been given at conferences, some to faculty workshops, some to convocations and classes, one or two have been published as periodical articles. This little book brings together such material in a largely rewritten form, and with a continuity of thought that occasional lectures lack.

It is an attempt to unfold the idea of a Christian college as I have come to understand it after teaching more than twenty years in such an institution. Nobody can invest his life that way, least of all a philosopher, without asking what he is doing and why. The outcome is therefore a philosophy of Christian liberal arts education written for the layman, not the philosopher. I have in mind teachers and students who are trying to articulate their own thinking on the subject, public relations officers and "friends of the college." I hope it may help orient such people to the Christian calling in which they are involved.

Like any philosophy of education it deals, if unobtrusively, with the foundations of education in human values (Chaps. 1 and 2), in the nature of man (Chap. 3) and in epistemology (Chaps. 4 and 5), as well as with such related topics as academic freedom, campus life and social consequences. The title of the work takes a little bravado, inspired as it is by John Henry Newman's *Idea of a University* and Elton Trueblood's *Idea of a College,* but I trust it will also indicate two of my sources of inspiration and guidance.

I wish to thank the respective editors for the use of material previously published as "Education, A Christian Calling" (Copyright 1962 by *Christianity Today*), "The Idea of a Christian College" (Copyright 1970 by *Christianity Today*), and "Is Academic Freedom Too Dangerous?" (*Eternity,* Feb. 1964). The last of these appeared concurrently in the *Bulletin* of Wheaton College. An earlier version of Chapter 5, "Experience Is Not Enough," appeared in *Universitas,* March 1974. To faculty and administrators at a dozen Christian liberal arts colleges, and to some of their students and my own, I am indebted for providing not only the occasions, but also the sympathetic hearing and critical encouragement that gave the overall project reason to be. Hudson T. Armerding, Donald Mitchell and Morris A. Inch read the manuscript and offered valuable suggestions; misconceptions and infelicitous expressions that remain are mine, not theirs. When Cynthia Koechling typed the manuscript for the second time, it included this acknowledgment that tells how sincerely I appreciate her help.

—Arthur F. Holmes

# The Idea
## of a
# Christian College

# 1 WHY A CHRISTIAN COLLEGE?

The French existentialist Jean-Paul Sartre describes man's predicament in the words, "Existence precedes essence." What he intends is that human existence comes devoid of any built-in value, any prior direction or inherent meaning. The naked fact that I am awakens me to the realization that if life is to mean anything at all, then I must myself create its meaning. I am free to make life what I will, dreadfully free, but I can also shrink from this responsibility and lapse into the empty anonymity of "bad faith."

In many basic regards I cannot agree with Sartre, for God has vested life with rich meaning and purpose, and the very fact of man's existence is inherently valuable at least to God. Man is not free to make of life whatever he will, nor to affirm values wholly alien to the created order. Yet Sartre has highlighted the predicament of modern man at a loss to know what life is all about.

Some analogy exists, I suggest, between that existential predicament (to which the final chapter will return) and the predicament of today's college student. The fact is that too many young people attend college or university, and their parents encourage them, without any gripping sense of what college is all about beyond tentative vocational goals or questionable social aspirations. Many attend Christian colleges for reasons that are so secondary, if not altogether inadequate, that they will end up frustrated unless they can find other meaning to their education, a meaning that is large enough to carry the weight of all that college involves.

The fact also is that public opinion saddles the Christian

college with inadequate reasons for existing, reasons the college cannot accept if it is to conceive and implement its task effectively and as a whole. Faulty expectations generate public relations problems and these add a needless burden to the problems of higher education today.

We face a generation of students for whom much in life has lost its meaning, for whom morality has lost its moorings, for whom education has lost its attraction. Add to this the economic crunch on small colleges and it becomes overwhelmingly obvious that we need to get down to basics, to the underlying and central reason for existing at all. Otherwise the student and the college may both lapse in "bad faith" into the faceless anonymity of people and places without distinctive meaning and become mere statistics in the educational almanac.

## AVOIDING PITFALLS

A frequent idea people have of the Christian college has been captured in the label "defender of the faith."[1] Though defending the faith was certainly an apostolic responsibility, it is hard to extend it to all of the educational task, all of art and science or all of campus life. Yet a defensive mentality is still common among pastors and parents; many suppose that the Christian college exists to protect young people against sin and heresy in other institutions. The idea therefore is not so much to educate as to indoctrinate, to provide a safe environment plus all the answers to all the problems posed by all the critics of orthodoxy and virtue.

This is an idea, I say—more a caricature than a reality. The trouble with it is that there often are no ready-made answers, new problems arise constantly, and the critics are perplexingly creative. The student who is simply conditioned to respond in certain ways to certain stimuli is at a loss when he confronts novel situations, as he will in a changing society undergoing a knowledge explosion. He needs a disciplined understanding of

---

[1] This designation was used in the Danforth Foundation study by M. M. Pattillo and D. M. MacKenzie, *Church-Sponsored Higher Education in the United States* (American Council on Education, 1966). The label and description were publicly rejected by a group of Christian colleges.

his heritage plus creativity, logical rigor and self-critical honesty, far more than he needs prepackaged sets of questions and answers. The mistake in cloistering young people to keep them from sin and heresy, as evangelicals—of all people—should realize, is that these things come ultimately not from the environment but out of the heart. And while every parent feels protective toward his youngsters, over-protectiveness can stifle faith and hope and love, and trigger opposite excesses of thought and conduct.

Is the idea of a Christian college, then, simply to offer a good education plus biblical studies in an atmosphere of piety? These are desirable ingredients, but are they the essence of the idea? After all, through religious adjuncts near a secular campus, students could be offered biblical studies and support for personal piety while they were getting a good education, without all the money and manpower and facilities and work involved in maintaining a Christian college.

Nor is the idea of a Christian liberal arts college to train people for church-related vocations, desirable as this may be as a by-product and central as it may be elsewhere in the educational work of the church. Training, in contrast to education, develops skills and techniques for handling given materials and facts and situations. Education admittedly includes some training in the earlier stages of learning. But the educated man shows independence and creativity of mind to fashion new skills and techniques, new patterns of thought. He has acquired research ability, the power to gather, sift and manipulate new facts and materials, and to handle altogether novel situations. The educated Christian exercises critical judgment and manifests the ability to interpret and to evaluate information, particularly in the light of the Christian revelation. In a word, if he is to act creatively and to speak with cogency and clarity to the minds of his fellows, the educated Christian must be at home in the world of ideas and men. Christians, unfortunately, often talk to themselves. We think in ruts, and express ourselves in a familiar kind of family jargon. Unless we understand the thought- and value-patterns of our day, as well as those of biblical revelation and the Christian community, and unless we speak fluently the language of our contemporaries, we tragically limit our effectiveness.

Another inadequate reason is the social and extracurricular benefits of the Christian college. It is true that in a small institution one has closer relations with both students and faculty, and that in a Christian institution one expects to find Christian friends                          . It is also true that one stands a better chance of becoming a campus leader or working in student publications or proving athletic prowess. But these are only fringe benefits; however much they contribute to the student's personal development, they are secondary to his education as such. Many of them can be matched outside of college, for it does not take four years out of the work force at a cost over $14,000 plus lost earnings in order to play soccer, to chair a committee, to find a mate, to put on a rocking-chair marathon, or even to give Christian witness by serving with love in the local old folks home. These things can be done without ever going to college.

College is for education, the liberal arts college for a liberal education, and the Christian college for a Christian education. These are the basics to which we must get back. To sell college primarily on some other basis is to operate under false pretenses; and to start into college for some other reason is to ask for frustrations. We must therefore come to see education as a Christian calling, we must explore what "liberal education" means and how it is affected by the Christian's task.

Then why a Christian college? Its distinctive should be an education that cultivates the creative and active integration of faith and learning, of faith and culture. This is its unique task in higher education today. While the reality is often more like an *interaction* of faith and learning, a dialog, than a completely ideal integration, it must under no circumstance become a *disjunction* between piety and scholarship, faith and reason, religion and science, Christianity and the arts, theology and philosophy, or whatever the differing points of reference may be. The Christian college will not settle for a militant polemic against secular learning and science and culture, as if there were a great gulf fixed between the secular and the sacred. All truth is God's truth, no matter where it is found, and we can thank him for it all.

Integration also transcends awkward *conjunctions* of faith and learning in some unholy alliance rather than a fruitful union. What we need is not Christians who are also scholars but Christian scholars, not Christianity alongside education but Christian education. This precludes taking critical potshots at variant interpretations of material without working out a more satisfactory explanation. It shuns tacked-on moralizing and applications, stale and superficial approaches that fail to penetrate the real intellectual issues. It requires a thorough analysis of methods and materials and concepts and theoretical structures, a lively and rigorous interpenetration of liberal learning with the content and commitment of Christian faith. The Christian college has a constructive task, far more than a defensive one.

## THE EDUCATIONAL DISTINCTIVE

The task is distinctive for two reasons. In the first place it is distinct from other Christian involvement in higher education. The Christian college is of course only one way of making the Christian presence felt academically. In the secular university, Christian students and professors walk a different road, primarily that of witnessing in a non-Christian environment. But important as this is—in fact the Christian college should encourage some of its finest students to become Christian professors and Christian scholars in secular academia—the primary impact is still a *conjunction* of Christian witness with secular education rather than the integration of faith and learning into an education that is itself Christian. The Christian college, moreover, is primarily an undergraduate teaching institution, not primarily a graduate school, nor a collection of professional schools, nor a research and public service institution as the modern university has become. Its task is far more specific.

The Bible institute and Bible college offer another way. They came into being to provide biblical instruction for Christian laymen so as to make their witness and their church work more effective, and they have become undergraduate training schools for Christian workers. They have obvious value, but the most they can achieve is conjunctive rather than integrative. To enlarge a person's biblical and theological knowledge and to train him for Christian service is not the same thing as helping him to work in the arts and sciences and to understand all of life from a Christian perspective.

Programs of biblical studies have recently been established by evangelicals on or near a few secular campuses in order to instruct the Christian and to engage the non-Christian in dialog. These programs range from a Bible-institute type of instruction for undergraduates (as in Urbana, Illinois) to graduate-level religious studies offered by scholars who might also teach in the university (as at Regent College in Vancouver, B.C.). But again the impact is primarily conjunctive and only occasionally integrative. Apart from the occasional Christian scholar teaching in a secular university in a non-theological discipline, the integration of faith and learning remains the distinctive task of the Christian liberal arts college.

Some Christian institutions give themselves primarily or largely to professional or vocational training. The seminary, for instance, devotes itself to the professional preparation of college graduates for various types of church-related ministry, and other Christian institutions offer vocational preparation in such areas as business, education and home economics. We shall comment later, in Chapters 3 and 8, about the relation of vocational training to liberal education, but one obvious difference is already apparent: the vocational is more concerned to provide the knowledge and skills needed for a particular set of tasks, while the latter is concerned with other qualities of a liberally educated person and, in a Christian college, with the development of Christian perspectives in all areas of life and thought. What commends the liberal arts college is that the Christian's vocation is larger by far than any specific ministry or vocation he may enter: it reaches into everything a person is and can be or do.

## THE RELIGIOUS DISTINCTIVE

The Christian college is distinctive, in the second place, because we live in a secular society that compartmentalizes religion and treats it as peripheral or even irrelevant to large areas of life and thought. Public education and large segments of private education are consequently thoroughly secular. The Hebrew-Christian world-view that once gave meaning and value to all of Western life and thought has disintegrated. The medieval university was governed by a unifying religious perspective but education today is rootless, or at best governed by pragmatism and the heterogeneity of viewpoints that makes ours both a secular and a pluralistic society. The result is a *multi*versity not a *uni*versity, an institution without a unifying world-view and so without unifying educational goals.[2]

The Christian college refuses to compartmentalize religion. It retains a unifying Christian world-view and brings it to bear in understanding and participating in the various arts and sciences, as well as in non-academic aspects of campus life. Its oldest precedent is the medieval university, where the life and thought of the entire community were penetrated and informed by theological studies.

American higher education was the child of religion, and the history both of church denominations and of the westward expansion can be traced through the history of America's colleges and universities. Harvard, Yale, Princeton and Columbia—to name but a few—began this way, and the list of those established prior to the Civil War includes 49 founded by Presbyterians, 34 by Methodists, 25 by Baptists and 21 by Congregationalists.[3] Some of this number have become multiversities or lost their evangelical distinctives, but others are still known among evangelicals today as distinctively Christian colleges, among them Geneva College, Taylor University and Wheaton. Yet all of them began with an eye to the propagation of religion and morality as well as for the sake of education and

---

[2] Clark Kerr, former President of the University of California, uses the term "multiversity" to indicate that it serves a variety of *uses* in contemporary society, a largely pragmatic notion. See his *The Uses of the University* (Harvard Univ. Press, 1963).

[3] D. G. Tewksbury, *The Founding of American Colleges and Universities Before the Civil War* (Columbia Univ., 1932; Archon Books, 1965), chap. II.

culture, and they at least conjoined scholarship with evangelical fervor and a quest for social righteousness, to whatever extent the two were effectively integrated. Over the years, various reasons for existence have been given, sometimes protective or apologetic, sometimes pietist or missionary, sometimes vocational. Yet underlying it all was the basic conviction that Christian perspectives can generate a world-view large enough to give meaning to all the disciplines and delights of life and to the whole of a liberal education.

Some observers have doubted whether the Christian college has any distinctive contribution to make at all, whether it is not too committed to offer a truly liberal education, whether it can survive the skyrocketing cost of private education and the competition of rapidly multiplying state universities and community colleges, or whether the church might not do better to put its resources of men and money behind some other enterprise on the secular campus.

I do not think for a moment that the situation is as black as some of these prophets declare, either in terms of our present contribution, or in terms of educational philosophy, or in terms of the economic prospects. I think rather that the Christian college has not sufficiently articulated its educational philosophy, and has not sold the evangelical public or perhaps even its own students and teachers on what it is trying to do. A few exceptions to this generalization have come from denominational schools with well-established views on the relation of Christianity to culture and a well-established scholarly heritage.[4] But by and large we have not dreamed large enough dreams or are confused about the values of liberal education or have forgotten the redemptive impact of faith on culture. In any case we are in integrity compelled to face basic questions. Why should the Christian college exist? Why choose to attend a Christian college? What meaning has Christian liberal arts education today?

---

[4] In particular see the Calvin College study, *Christian Liberal Arts Education* (Calvin College, 1970), and the St. Olaf College study, *Integration in the Christian Liberal Arts College* (St. Olaf College Press, 1956), although neither of these is addressed to the general public or to the student.

# 2 THEOLOGICAL FOUNDATIONS

Before we go any further into the idea of a Christian college we must pause and get our theological bearings. The Christian is not as radically free as Sartre maintains to do whatever he chooses and to create whatever meaning he can for his activities. Rather he is committed to thinking and acting as a Christian, that is to say, he will be guided by what he believes about God and his purposes for men. While this is of the utmost importance in shaping our ideas aright, it also faces head-on the uneasy feelings some Christians have about higher education—that it is "secular" and "worldly," that it endangers faith and devotion, that it is unimportant in comparison with all our other obligations, or that Christians have no business putting money and manpower into education that could be used to fulfil the missionary mandate of the church.

I have no intention of arguing that the Christian college is our only option. Far from it: we have seen that there are other worthwhile ways in which the Christian presence has been and is being felt in higher education. In fact the Christian liberal arts college is largely an American innovation, unknown in Europe and even in Canada. Rather I want in this chapter to unfold the biblical and theological mandate for Christian involvement in higher education in general, as well as for the Christian liberal arts college in particular. The discussion will focus on four concepts: creation, man, truth, and the cultural mandate.

## CREATION

Beginning with New Testament times and repeatedly since then,

21

the Christian church has been confronted by various kinds of Gnosticism. The Gnostic claimed that man is a creature of two worlds, matter and mind, that matter is the source of life's evils while mind is the source of what is rational and good, and that the two are locked in unending and unresolvable conflict.

Distortions like this often afford occasions for bringing the truth more clearly into focus, and so the apostle Paul, when faced with the Gnostic depreciation of bodily things, reminded the church that everything in existence is created by God and therefore is of value (I Tim. 4:1-5). He might well have had in mind the first chapter of Genesis, in which the term "good" is applied six times to various aspects of creation, and "very good" is finally applied to it all. Thereby God declares that all creation, both the part and the whole, is of value to him; Paul simply adds that as a result it should be valued by men as well. Sin occurs not when men enjoy created things but when they misuse them. The sin, in fact, is in not valuing as we should the resources God has made.

Another kind of Gnosticism has haunted the church in the past, and haunts both church and college to this day. It too claims that man is a creature of two worlds, this time the natural and the spiritual, the secular and the sacred, the world and the church. In each pair of terms the former indicates the source of life's evils, which is to be avoided as much as possible, and the latter is fundamentally incompatible with it. This kind of Gnosticism keeps the Christian from cultural involvement, from artistic appreciation and creativity, from political and social action, and it generates a misdirected fear of science and philosophy and human learning. It produces needless tensions between faith and culture, a defensive attitude and sometimes even outright anti-intellectualism.

Obviously terms like "natural," "secular" and "world" are ambiguous. What is natural for man—like his intellectual curiosity and artistic powers and political concerns—is not what the New Testament means by "the natural man," and not everything in this world has the bad moral and religious connotations of the New Testament term "worldly." The forgotten ingredient is that, for all human sin has done to distort the scene, this world is still God's creation, of value to both God and men. The "secular" is not itself evil; in fact, in God's world it too is sacred.

The biblical concept of creation imparts sanctity to all realms of nature and to the history and culture of man. This is my Father's world. To him it owes its existence and order, its developing structures and exciting possibilities. Everything in nature and in history plays its part in carrying out his purposes and in manifesting his glory. For the Christian neither nature nor history is self-originating, self-operating, self-sustaining or self-explanatory. We therefore approach the works of God, probe their mysteries, and harness their potentialities with humility but with boldness as well. The natural and social sciences lay before us old vistas and new horizons. In the humanities we grapple with ultimate questions and struggle to express our values and beliefs with a precision and beauty becoming the sanctity of life. To neglect the kind of education that helps us understand and appreciate God's world betrays either shallow thinking or fearful disbelief.

## MAN

That God made man in his own image reminds us that in a vast universe that reflects God's glory, man is uniquely "crowned with glory and honor." He is a person equipped by God with rational, moral and artistic powers to invest for his Maker. He is a sinner also, it is true, whose original image of God and personal powers are corrupted. But he is nonetheless the object of a divine providence that limits evil and preserves man's personality, and he is the object of a divine grace that restores God's image and sanctifies human powers for God's glory.

In other words, man has a God-given, God-preserved, God-restorable potential, a potential to be developed, disciplined and invested in response to God. Such development, discipline and direction are the Christian's responsibility and stewardship. To educate the whole person, to encourage disciplined learning and the quest for excellence is a sacred trust. The Christian should give himself contagiously to looking around him and to thinking, to the exploration of nature and to the transmission of a cultural heritage, as well as to teaching Christian beliefs and values. The educator's task is to inspire and equip individuals to think and act for themselves in the dignity of men created in God's image. There is no room here for a dichotomy between what is secular and what is sacred, for everything about men created in God's image belongs to God—that is, it is sacred.

Man is at heart a religious being. I use the word "heart" in its biblical sense in which a man's religious stance is at the "heart" of everything: from it flow all the issues of life. Religion cannot be compartmentalized; the secular man attempts to do so but succeeds only in fragmenting his life, unless he roots another religion at the heart of things, perhaps a quasi-religion of a humanistic or materialist sort.

But if man is at heart a religious being, then all his activities are animated and informed by his faith, be they intellectual or artistic, political or commercial. There can be no effective dichotomy of the secular and the sacred or of culture and faith. Paul tells us to do everything "heartily, as to the Lord" (Col. 3:23). The phrase is significant, for it is given in response to the Gnostic dualism that had confused the Colossian church by dichotomizing man.

Martin Luther once said that the shoemaker should shoe the sole of the Pope as religiously as the Pope should pray for the soul of the shoemaker. And the astronomer John Kepler: "I have completed a work of my calling with as much intellectual strength as Thou hast granted me. I have declared the praise of Thy works to the men who will read the evidence of it, so far as my finite spirit can comprehend them in their infinity."[1] In this sense at least, shoemaking and astronomy, and all our arts and sciences, become religious activities.

### TRUTH

If we confess that God is the all-wise Creator of all, then

---

[1] Quoted by Arnold Nash in *The University and the Modern World* (Macmillan, 1944), p. 257.

he has perfect knowledge of everything men ever sought to know or do. The truth about the physical order is known perfectly to him, the truth about man and society, and the truth about everything we ever wondered about in our most perplexed moments. The early church fathers summed this up in what has become a guidepost for Christian scholars ever since—*all truth is God's truth, wherever it be found.*

Once we grasp this principle, then the worlds of literature, philosophy, history, science and art become the Christian's rightful domain. Of course not everything writers and scientists and others declare can be true; some of it is patently false and some less patently so. Yet truth shows up all over the place, fragmentarily perhaps and with pervasive misinterpretation, and God the Creator is ultimately the source of all that is true.

A second principle is the *unity of truth.* When the apostle writes that in Christ "are hid all the treasures of wisdom and knowledge" (Col. 2:3), he refers not only to the divine omniscience but also to what he explained in the previous chapter, that Jesus Christ is God Incarnate, the Creator and Lord of every created thing. All our knowledge of anything comes into focus around that fact. We see nature, man, society, and the arts and sciences in proper relationship to their divine Creator and Lord. This facilitates an overall philosophy that accords not with pagan principles but with Christ (Col. 2:8). The truth is a coherent whole by virtue of the common focus that ties it all into one.

The Christian college explores truth focused in that way. The pursuit of truth, as pagans like Plato as well as the biblical writers recognized, carries with it certain moral prerequisites: the willingness and determination to learn, intellectual honesty, a self-discipline that makes lesser and more selfish satisfactions wait. But while such dedication is prerequisite to learning, a Christian understanding of things is not thereafter achieved by some mystical illumination unrelated to rational considerations. The Holy Spirit illuminates the Christian mind by witnessing to the truth taught by the Scriptures, not independently thereof and not without the intellectual work involved in studying the biblical revelation and understanding Christian theology.

The Christian regards the biblical revelation as his final rule of faith and conduct, but he does not think of it as an exhaustive source of all truth. The teaching authority of Scripture commits the believer at certain focal points and so provides an interpretive framework, an overall glimpse of how everything relates to God, but there is no royal road to learning and no alternative to disciplined intellectual inquiry if we would find out about nature or man or God. Moreover, if all truth is God's truth and truth is one, then God does not contradict himself, and in the final analysis there will be no conflict between the truth taught in Scripture and truth available from other sources.

The relation between reason and revelation is therefore in principle no more antithetical than the relation between culture and the church. That God has revealed himself in Scripture means among other things that he has given us a true and reliable source of knowledge, sufficient for its intended purposes, but we cannot understand that revelation and grasp the knowledge it imparts without *thinking* about it. Revelation by whatever means affords a *source* of knowledge and an impetus to learning; reason is a God-given capacity for *understanding* and organizing and using what is revealed. Revelation and reason are both God-given, both to be valued and used.

Faith is neither a way of knowing nor a source of knowledge. Faith is rather a man's openness and wholehearted response to God's self-revelation. It does not preclude thinking either about what we believe or about what we are unsure of, nor does it make it unnecessary to search for truth or to examine evidence and arguments. Faith does not cancel out created human activities; rather it motivates, purges and guides them. It devotes "all my being's ransomed powers," including reason, to God. Like any gift the intellect can be misused, but it is still God's gift, intended by him to be fully enjoyed and rightly appropriated within the context of a living faith.

For the evangelical in education, therefore, Christian commitment does not restrict intellectual opportunity and endeavor, but rather it fires and inspires him to purposeful learning. Christian education should not blindfold the student's eyes to all the world has to offer, but it should open them to truth wherever it may be found, truth that is ultimately unified in and derived from God. It should be a liberating experience that enlarges horizons, deepens insight, sharpens the mind, exposes new areas of inquiry and sensitizes our ability to appreciate the good and the beautiful as well as the true.

What I have said about truth and intellectual inquiry could be said also about goodness and the concern for social justice. All goodness, justice, love and every virtue come ultimately from God. Every good thing comes from the Father, and St. Paul therefore encourages us to think about "whatsoever things" are just and virtuous as well as true (Phil. 4:8).

Something similar can be said for the beautiful and for the creative arts, for Paul adds the lovely or "pleasing" to the true and the good. Certainly God created man's capacity for aesthetic enjoyment, he made the world that delights and awes us, and he made us artistically creative. In this sense, then, all beauty and creativity is God's, to be enjoyed and dedicated to him. None of our cultural endeavors is excluded, nor can they be from education that is Christian.

## THE CULTURAL MANDATE

At creation God made man in his own image, to steward his own and nature's resources creatively and wisely. Man's cultural responsibilities originate here. Tensions occur between faith and culture, it is true, some of which are due to our inability to grasp relationships and see life's task as a whole, and others of which are due to the imperfections of particular cultures. Nothing in the cultural mandate makes twentieth-century American culture, or any other culture, sacrosanct; every culture stands constantly under the judgment of God. But cultural responsibilities persist; they began with creation.

We read in Scripture of the agriculture and art and technology that men developed, of the cities they built and the nations of which they were part. We read of social justice and compassion provided for in the Jewish law, preached by the prophets, and practiced at times by the kings. We read of the virtue of conscientious work, the joys of song and of love and friendship.

We read the Old Testament poetic books whose artistic form is that of their culture. In the New Testament we meet one who incarnated himself in the mundane, in the social and religious and political structures of the time. He spent thirty of his thirty-two earthly years in "secular" pursuits, in the family at Nazareth and at the carpenter's bench. From the parables he told we sense his delight in nature and in Jewish culture. He says that all of life is a stewardship, sacred before God. We meet the apostles who talk of the Lordship of Christ in everything, and in their missionary work use cultural vehicles, even Greek philosophical concepts, to communicate the gospel.

Man is a cultural being. God made him to be that way and there is no escape from cultural involvement and cultural tasks. Even a counterculture itself becomes a culture, or else it blends back into the culture it condemns. Occasionally a religious community tries to stand outside culture, but it develops into a subculture with its own cultural tasks.

Culture was ordained by God. The creation mandate to replenish and subdue and have dominion has never been rescinded. It may be argued that man's sin changes things and perverts culture, so that God's grace calls man out of culture to witness to it rather than participate in it. Yet the biblical cases of cultural involvement all occurred after the fall. In fact Psalm 8 defines the uniqueness of man in terms of the cultural mandate given in Genesis 1, and Hebrews 2 reiterates the Psalmist's words. In response to the complaint that man has sinned and thereby failed culturally, the epistle to the Hebrews speaks of the redemptive work of Christ, later of men who did wide varieties of things "by faith" (Heb. 11), and of the believer's relationship to such cultural things as marriage and money and political authority (Heb. 13).

The point is that God's goodness as well as man's sin affects culture. Theologians speak of the "common grace" of a God who makes the sun to shine on the just and the unjust alike, and preserves among fallen men a measure of civil justice and social order and a degree of human love and compassion. Fallen men, whether they want it or not and however distortedly, still image their Creator. The mathematical genius of an Einstein and the artistic creativity of a Picasso are God's gifts to mankind through common grace.

But God's redeeming grace also affects culture, for the men he makes whole are cultural beings whose activities are now directly affected by the truth and love of God. They bear witness by their lives, and that includes their arts and sciences, to the God in whose image they are being re-created. God's grace affects a culture through the cultural penetration of those his grace redeems.

To confess God as Creator and Christ as Lord is thus to affirm his hand in all life and thought. It is to admit that every part of the created order is sacred, and that the Creator calls us to exhibit his wisdom and power both by exploring the creation and developing its resources and by bringing our own created abilities to fulfilment. For while all nature declares the glory of God, we men uniquely image the Creator in our created creativity. Implicit in the doctrine of creation is a cultural mandate and a call to the creative integration of faith with learning and culture. It is a call, not just to couple piety with intellect, nor just to preserve biblical studies in our school, but more basically to see every area of thought and life in relation to the wisdom and will of God and to replenish the earth with the creativity of human art and science.

Plainly, the four theological concepts we have considered affect the values we find in education and liberal learning. To reject their values is to flirt with Gnosticism. The Christian college accepts and helps to realize them in the lives of its students. All of life with its culture and its learning must be penetrated with Christian perspectives, if Jesus Christ is to be Lord of all. All of a young person's human potential must be as fully developed as possible, if the stewardship of his life is to honor God. The Christian has a mandate in education.

# 3 THE LIBERAL ARTS: WHAT AND WHY?

A typical college student sat in my office. He had come to preregister, and beneath his hesitation I detected confusion about the purpose of his education. Should he take another literature course, or something in accounting? Why the history of philosophy or of art, or of anything else for that matter? He was majoring also in psychology, but why experimental psychology or personality theory when what he wanted was to understand people so as to communicate more effectively? What would he ever *do* with all this stuff anyway: literature, history, philosophy, experimental psychology? Whatever *use* does it have in "real life," and in particular for the Christian?

I could have taken several approaches. I could have asked, Socratic style, "What do you mean by *real* life?" And I might have led him to see that literature and history and philosophy and psychology deal with reality to a larger extent and in deeper dimensions than any collection of "how to do it" courses. I could have talked about the cultural mandate under which the first task of mankind to which God's grace has restored us as Christians is to glorify God in all our creatureliness, and therefore to understand the creation and with heart and mind to join in the cultural undertaking of the human race. I could simply have pontificated that this is a liberal arts college and he should get a liberal education. But not being sure he would understand the implications of that, I suggested instead that his was the wrong question to ask about education.

## ASKING THE RIGHT QUESTION

We are reminded by those who try to buffer us against "future shock" that our present job-skills will soon be outmoded, and that the things we learn to do now will be vastly different in a few short years. Education should therefore prepare us to adapt, to think, to be creative. Whether these prophets exaggerate or not, it is also true that the "I" who in a few short years will "do something in real life" will by then be a different "I" from the "I" who now takes a course in college. My personality is not static but dynamic, growing, changing. The question to ask about education, then, is not "What can I do with all this stuff anyway?" because both I and my world are changing, but rather "What will all this stuff do to me?" This question is basic to the concept of liberal education.

When I began to teach, someone reminded me that the verb "to teach" carries a double object. Teaching is like telling: I have just told a story about a student, but I have also told you. When people ask what I teach, I sometimes say "philosophy," but sometimes (and partly to tease them) I say "students." For the question a teacher must ask about his teaching is not "What can they do with it?" but rather "What will it do to them? What sort of men and women will they become by wrestling with this material in the way I present it? And what sort of materials and methods could I develop to help them become more fully the people they are capable of being?"

Now this "whatever-can-I-do-with-all-this-stuff" question comes up in various disguises. Perhaps the most frequent is the vocational: what will history and literature and philosophy contribute to my work as a businessman, a doctor, an engineer or a minister? Liberal education contributes far more than is sometimes supposed to many vocations, and more will be said of this in the final chapter. Moreover, we must never underestimate the importance of work; its value in the order of creation is far greater than the value of earning a living. A man's daily work, whatever it is, should be an offering to God (Eph. 6:5-9), as well as a service to others and a means to his own personal growth and dignity. This biblical approach to work is vastly different from the aristocratic attitude of Aristotle and some of the Greeks who unduly elevated the life of the mind in contrast to more mundane tasks. But to realize this is to uncover the fallacy in a purely vocational approach to education. The human vocation is far larger than the scope of any job a person may hold because we are human persons created in God's image, to honor and serve God and men in all we do, not just in the way we earn a living.

None of us wants the kind of dehumanized brave new world that manufactures men and women to fill jobs. Our technological society has been indicted of late for making productivity the purpose of society, rather than people. Yet the same indictment could be leveled against the view that education is job training, for it too has sold out to the productivity principle by subordinating what people are to what they do. A person is not just *homo faber,* man who makes things. If he were just a worker, vocational training would suffice; but since he is more than a worker it follows that vocational training is not enough.

Vocations and jobs are made for men, not men for vocations and jobs. The question to ask about an education is *not* "What can I do with it?", but rather "What is it doing to me—as a person?" Education has to do with the making of persons, Christian education with the making of Christian persons. Since this is what God's creative and redemptive work is about—the making of persons in his own image—it follows that an education that helps make us more fully persons is especially important to Christians.

### DEFINITIONS

What is liberal education that makes it larger and more enriching than vocational preparation? What do we mean by the liberal arts? A term may be defined by its extension or by its intension. To define by extension, we identify the class of particular things to which a term refers. The term "man" extends to Tom, Dick, Harry, Mary, Jane, Sue—the whole gamut. To define by intension, we try to capture the concept involved, the underlying nature that all members of that class have in common, the essence of it.

An extensional definition of the liberal arts would refer to a set of academic disciplines. In the Middle Ages the term referred to a trivium plus a quadrivium of disciplines. The initial three concerned the art of language and were grammar, rhetoric and logic; the four (geometry, arithmetic, music and astronomy) were regarded as essentially mathematical and taught the art of reasoning and abstract thought.

So the liberal arts were a group of disciplines having to do with language and thinking, and something of the intension of the term emerges as a result. Along with these liberal arts were disciplines like theology and law, which not only equipped men to serve God and society but also provided the subject matter for their rational inquiry. Theology and science rapidly became part of the liberal arts. By the time we get to the eighteenth and nineteenth century, the extension of the liberal arts broadens and becomes synonymous with classical education, so that you are not liberally educated without Latin and Greek and classical literature, and unless you can write Latin poetry and give speeches in classical languages. For a while it included natural philosophy (science), moral philosophy (ethics and political science) and mental philosophy (logic and metaphysics), so that to this day the "Doctor of Philosophy" degree can be earned in almost any discipline. In the twentieth century, there has been a tendency to equate the liberal arts with a broad, general education that ranges across the natural sciences, the social sciences and the humanities, and religion is increasingly considered as one of the liberal arts.

Whatever the disciplines cited, extensional definitions are insufficient. They refer to the changing content of human knowledge rather than to the purpose for which one learns, so that students still ask, *"Why* do we have to learn this stuff anyway?"* and *"Why* is this important?"* If liberal education is equated with general education, then the liberally educated person is one who has dabbled in a promiscuous variety of things. Such a scope is insufficient either to fully motivate students or to justify itself, because it is hopelessly fragmented. It might allow the principle that all truth is God's truth wherever it is found, but it disregards the unity of truth. It does nothing to unify a man or his view of life, and it might well encourage the conclusion that life has no overall meaning at all. It simply creates a connoisseur of the fragments of life. But a jack of all trades is a master of none: he is a fragmented individual. What today we label as general education requirements do not themselves make for the unified understanding that education desires.

To see what we mean by liberal education we have to get beyond extensional to intensional definitions and grasp the unifying essence of the thing. Cicero suggested that liberal education is the education of men for freedom, the education of free men for the exercise of their freedom rather than of slaves. Aristotle leaves the impression that education is for the wise use of one's leisure, for free men are leisured men who do not have to work but are in a position to exercise political and social leadership. In that sense liberal education becomes education for leadership, and in that spirit the early American college emphasized preparation for the leadership exercised by the professions, hence a non-professional preparation for the professions through developing a man's rational powers. More recently the stress has been on education for citizenship in a democracy. Here again the conception is of a free man and a role he must play in life beyond his remunerative work.

In all of this, the needed clue is that the liberal arts are those which are appropriate to man as man, rather than to man in his specific function as a worker or as a professional or even as a scholar. A man may be all of these things, but he is more basically man. It was Cicero who defined the liberal arts as those which are appropriate to humanity. If man is to be anything more than a half-human specialist or technician, if a man is to feel life whole and to live it whole rather than piecemeal, if he is to think for himself rather than live secondhand, the liberal arts are needed to educate the person. There is no difficulty in transferring this clue concerning liberal education to a Christian conception of man. Man is created in the image of God. We are to image God in all of our creaturely activities, our cultural existence and every phase of our humanity. To image God in the fulness of our humanity is our highest calling. A liberal education that develops our humanity therefore implements God's calling, and the creation mandate finds expression in the educational process.

In his classic nineteenth-century work, *The Idea of a Uni-*

*versity,* John Henry Newman distinguishes between liberal and useful arts. It is not a complete disjunction, for the liberal arts are also useful, and the useful arts are based on liberal arts and sciences. But the point is that some arts are more liberal than others, and some more useful to man for economic and other particular purposes than they are of value to man as such. The distinction is worth preserving. It is the distinction between intrinsic and instrumental value. Some things have little but instrumental value: a shining new coin with the head of George Washington on one side and the American eagle on the other has instrumental worth: it is good for what you can buy with it but little else. If you tell me it is of intrinsic worth and you value it for itself, I call you a miser. Other things have far more intrinsic worth as well as some instrumental value. Understanding is valued for itself. Beauty and goodness are of value in themselves. In addition to the fact that beauty may have some utilitarian function and that it pays to be good and that knowledge can be useful, in addition to their instrumental worth, is their intrinsic worth. Liberal learning concerns itself with truth and beauty and goodness, which have intrinsic worth to men considered as persons rather than as workers or in whatever function alone.

We may distinguish along these lines between literature as one of the liberal arts and journalism in which the *use* of what is written predominates; between the natural sciences as man's quest to understand nature, which is liberal learning, and the technology that does something else with it; between political science on the one hand as the attempt to understand political institutions and processes, and propaganda techniques on the other; between the science of psychology and the useful art of counseling; between theology and the work of evangelism; between philosophy as a liberal art and apologetics as one use it might have. Usefulness is no crime. But the practical uses of things we learn are limited and changeable, while the effect of learning on the person is less limited because it lasts. Liberal learning therefore takes the long-range view and concentrates on what shapes a person's understanding and values rather than on what he can use in one or two of the changing roles he might later play.

The question to ask about education is not "What can I do with it?" That is the wrong question because it concentrates on instrumental values and reduces everything to a useful art. The right question to ask is rather "What can it do to me?"

## WHAT IS MAN?

Starting with this clue, what do the liberal arts contribute to the making of a man? This depends on the prior question: "What is man?" Here the Christian and the Christian college must be extremely careful. If you take a Freudian or a Marxist or a pragmatist or a behavioristic view of man, your conception of education will be geared accordingly. What then is man? Three essential aspects of our human identity are basic for Christian higher education. The list may not be exhaustive, although other aspects may well be embraced in this rubric. Nor do these three aspects correlate with a Greek or Enlightenment psychology that separates the three faculties of reason, will and emotion from each other. Faculty psychology has been outmoded by recent psychology and faulted by biblical theology, both of which require a more unified conception of personality such that the person as a whole thinks and chooses and feels and acts: thinking can proceed neither without choosing goals and assumptions nor without emotion. In the following account each of the three aspects characterizes the person as a whole and is inseparably intertwined with the others.

First, man is *a rational being*. I do not intend by this the Enlightenment conception of reason as unimpassioned and un-committed, detached and neutral on matters of faith and value, so that from universally clear and distinct ideas we infer necessarily and demonstrably true conclusions. Something of the sort may occur in mathematics, but it is relatively localized. In other areas we are more limited: "we see through a glass darkly," and "we know in part." Yet, as Aristotle said, all men by nature desire to know, we are inquisitive, we wonder. Too often our God-given intellectual curiosity has been deadened in earlier education, or thinking has been transformed into an idle spectator sport. The first task of liberal education is to fan the spark and ignite this native inquisitiveness.

To be rational is also to be analytic. Inquisitiveness leads us to examine more and more closely what is going on. "How does this happen? What do you mean? How can this be?" Reasoning is asking what and why and how. It asks about the meaning of life and probes the mysteries of our existence. It seeks understanding. Man has to ask questions and probe analytically, he has to learn to think and to think critically for himself, because this is part of what it is to be human.

To be rational is also to see things in relationship, to organize ideas into an ordered whole, to be systematic, to work toward a unified understanding. Three educational implications follow. First, interdisciplinary approaches to learning are important. Second, theoretical questions are unavoidable because man alone in creation is a theorizing being who extrapolates beyond the known and speculates about the unknown, formulates hypotheses for science to explore and imagines new worlds for art to create. Third, world-views must be examined and shaped, for man still strives to see things whole, however imperfectly he envisions that unity of truth which he seeks.

Bertrand Russell suggests that education has two purposes: to form the mind and to train the citizen. The Athenians, he says, concentrated on the former but the Spartans on the latter. The Spartans won but the Athenians were remembered. To form the mind, to stretch the understanding, to sharpen one's intellectual powers, to enlarge the vision, to cultivate the imagination and impart a sense of the whole—this is the task of liberal education.

If God, too, is rational and man struggles within the limitations of his creatureliness to think God's thoughts after him, then the rational life has religious significance. Like all of human existence, thinking has religious roots and proceeds from the heart; in the final analysis it is a man's religion that unifies his understanding. To the Christian in the Christian college, then, the development of rational inquiry becomes an expression of faith and hope and love addressed to God. It is part of man's response to God's self-revelation.

Intellectual development requires that we read and write. Reading is of course prerequisite to informed conversation, an art that is often sadly underdeveloped today. Writing is prerequisite to exactness of thought and expression. They accomplish what "discussion" alone can never achieve, unless it is constantly monitored and analyzed by an unusually competent teacher who forces the discussants to think and then to reshape their thoughts in more and more consistent and cogent and lucid ways. To read is to gain input, to fertilize thought, to objectify, to conceptualize, to follow an argument, to evaluate. To write is to become articulate, to express what I feel and explain why I feel as I do, to expound, to argue, to offer good reasons, to explore relationships, to have a sense of the whole, to see things in total context. To teach a person to read and to write is to teach him to think for himself, to develop more fully the possession of his God-given powers. He becomes in fact, not just in possibility, a rational being.

Second, man is *a historical being* with a past, present and future. Young people tend to turn off the past, but thereby they lose the sense of their own identity, for the present and the future are what they are in relation to the past. We have knowledge of the past only insofar as the past again becomes present and is known and understood and relived now in our minds. And the past shapes the present and future, so that we are what we are and where we are, and are heading where we are, because of the past. To understand our present and influence our future, then, we must grasp our past.

The existentialist reminds us that man is not merely a product of historical processes, stretching uniformly from the remote past into the distant future, but also an agent who transcends his past by acting to shape his future. This capacity for self-transcendence distinguishes man from the things he uses and from the rest of nature, for natural forces are not free so to act. To say that man is a historical being means that he participates in his own history, shaping his times and helping create his future. A man can transcend what he is now and act to make himself what he is not yet.

As such a historical agent, he is in the image of his Maker.

God, too, transcends the purely natural processes and outcomes of the created order when he acts in history and in the affairs and lives of men. By our creative action, we image the creativity of God. Liberal education that helps people develop into free agents who participate creatively in history is therefore a sacred task. It helps a person understand his history and develop a sense of direction, it contributes to far-sighted and wise decisions, it leads to intelligent and strategic action. For in order to act intelligently we must know where we are now and where, apart from our action, we are likely going.

Two educational goals follow. One is a critical appreciation of the past. Appreciation is positive: it captures the continuity of a heritage from the past into the present. But I say "critical appreciation" because unless we see the limitations of our past we will never be motivated to transcend those limitations in shaping our future. Critical appreciation of our past will free us to see creative possibilities for the future. The other goal is therefore creative participation in the future. I say "in the future" for two reasons. One is that the present is an abstraction. As soon as I say "now" it is past: all that we really have is the past and the future, and the future glides into the past. The other reason is that by politicizing the university as the locus of revolution, the activist generation of students involved itself too deeply in the present. Involvement in the now has its values, educational and otherwise, but the "now" becomes the "then" and leaves us unprepared for the future. We must keep an eye on the historical role for which man is created, whether he fulfils that role as churchman, parent or citizen, as scientist, teacher or businessman. As a historical agent he will inevitably participate in his future, and liberal education can help him do so with intelligence and creativity.

Third, man is *a valuing being*. We make value judgments and act to realize our values. The theological foundations of the last chapter brought the *value* of higher education into focus. A world-view that ties our thinking together and gives direction to what we do is not simply a theoretical system of value-neutral propositions, but a valuational orientation to life. It expresses what we hope as well as what we think; it says what we love and what we desire. If a man values the truth, he speaks it; if he values justice, he works for it; if he has hope amidst life's turmoil, his life has meaning. A man values peace and justice, love and beauty, community and solitude. He expresses his values in his arts and sciences, his political life, his social institutions, in the very history he creates. In the humanities— literature, the arts, philosophy, history—human values become explicit. The value a man places on various aspects of life comes out in the literature he writes. Read Hemingway or Tolstoi or Brecht and grapple with their views, for literature and the arts are a laboratory of life: one does not need to experiment with drugs and sex and violence in order to understand life's experiences and emotions for himself.

Values are more than feelings. By now the emotivist theory of value should be dead and can be buried, for it has been taken to pieces by philosophers who have shown beyond doubt that valuing also involves reasons that can be argued and generalized. Yet experience-oriented young people still seem to reduce values to feelings: a thing is right that you feel right about. It is "right for me." The result, as C. S. Lewis shows in his *Abolition of Man,* is a thorough relativism. For the Christian theist, values are more than feelings and they are not all relative; they have their basis in the very nature of what a man is in God's creation and so in the wisdom and the will of God. We image our Creator as valuing beings, for he, too, values: he loves, he delights, he seeks to realize the values he invested in his creation, and our values must follow from his.

Another educational goal accordingly follows, to teach values as well as facts. Somewhere in the curriculum, the student should be exposed to ethics, to aesthetics and other areas of value, and to the logical structure of value judgments. How do I make a moral judgment that is not a simple case of black or white, of obvious right or wrong? Are the consequences of an action all that matters (its instrumental value) or are some things intrinsically better than others? In a Christian college one must come to see the distinctive ingredients and bases of Christian values, and will hopefully make those values his own.

Man is at least a rational, historical and valuing being, and a liberal education is one that develops his capacity in these regards. It is perhaps significant that these three have all been associated with freedom in man. By acting rationally, Kant argued, we act free from the constraint of appetite and inclination. By historical action we are free to transcend our present condition. By valuing we reach beyond the actualities that otherwise hold us in their grip. Liberal education prepares a man for the wise exercise of the God-given freedom he can enjoy.

Perhaps other aspects should be considered as well. We have not distinguished man's religious nature, for, as we pointed out in Chapter 2, it is the very heart of his being from which everything else stems. The religious dimension of life is lived in and through the rational life, the historical action and the values that are our own.

What of the physical and the social? If we were after a list of activities or courses that liberal education should embrace, then it would probably be important to list them separately. But we have tried to avoid extensional definitions because they lead to fragmented general education listings, in favor of the intensional definition of liberal education as having to do with what is intrinsically and distinctively human. While there are other physical and social creatures than men, man's physical and social activities are simply means whereby he exercises the rational, historical and valuational nature that marks him off from beasts.

The physical provides a necessary but insufficient condition of all a man is and does in this life, and it should be valued and developed accordingly. But by definition, liberal education should concern itself with physical education as with other curricular areas in relationship to the goals of liberal education. That is, the primary concern will not be with physical skill or strength or stamina, but with the development of the person— his emotional balance and self-understanding, his ability to act decisively and creatively, his values. The measure of a man is neither his athletic prowess nor his lack thereof. It is other characteristics that make a man truly man. Physical training will not automatically either enhance these characteristics or detract from them, although it can contribute in either direction.

Plato said that excessive emphasis on athletics without literature or philosophy produces a pretty uncivilized type with no use for reasoned conviction, whose life is one of clumsy ignorance unrelieved by grace or beauty; whereas a purely academic life without athletic training leaves a man with little backbone. He seems on the right track, but he forgets that some sports are also arts, creative and beautiful, so that the athlete may well learn to understand and appreciate aesthetic values rather than simply acquiring strength, skill, self-reliance and a team spirit. In any case the Christian college must not only value highly the body God made but also teach physical education in a humanizing and liberating way, whether the values are aesthetic or moral and social, or whether the end-product is decisive action based on carefully argued plans.

Man's social nature must be cultivated without drifting into the extremes of individualism or collectivism. More will be said of this in the last two chapters of the book in relation to the college community and to today's world. The social, like the physical, is a necessary but insufficient precondition for rational, historical and valuing beings. Rational inquiry is not carried on in isolation but in dialog with other minds of the past and present: because it builds on their work, it is a social undertaking. Historical understanding and participation are both social, for a man's past and future are inevitably intertwined with the culture and the social institutions of which he is, thus far at least, a part. Our values are in large measure acquired from parents and peers and others, they are implemented in whatever social groups we belong to, and we seek to transmit them to others. Man's social nature is thus part and parcel of all the rest. To that extent at least, the goals of liberal education will include not only self-understanding, but also an understanding of other people and of social institutions and processes. This is essential in preparing men and women for participation in society, whether through marriage or through citizenship activities or through business and professional relationships.

Liberal education is an open invitation to join the human race and become more fully human. Its general goals include the ability to read and write and thereby think independently, a critical appreciation of the past and creative participation in the future, and an appreciation of lasting values coupled with the ability to make sound value judgments and live by them. Generalizations of this sort can readily be translated into objectives for different disciplines, so that the science professor will stress an understanding and appreciation of methods and concepts, and the historical development of his science and its cultural ramifications, rather than stressing technique alone or making the student into a narrow specialist. A considerable degree of specialization is of course appropriate in any major field of concentration, sufficient to prepare the student for graduate work in a highly competitive situation, but the liberal arts college has no business producing narrow specialists who see no further than their laboratory, and who have no sense of history and little understanding of science as an essentially human and cultural undertaking. It would be inexcusable nowadays for a Christian college to teach science without discussing the moral and social problems it has raised. Similarly the art teacher will work toward an understanding and appreciation of the creative process, of aesthetic values and the history and social role of art, for artists like scientists can become narrowly specialized technicians.

Liberal education is an opportunity to become more fully a human person in the image of God, to see life whole rather than fragmented, to transcend the provincialism of our place in history, our geographic location or our job. Provincialism isolates us from our past, isolates us from segments of the human race; cultural provincialism isolates the American way of life from anything else; vocational provincialism limits the horizon to a certain kind of task. But liberal education is an opportunity to become whole and to see life whole rather than provincially, fragmented in one way or another. It is an opportunity to find meaning for everything I am and do. Christian liberal arts education is concerned that we do this in the light of God's self-revelation, so that we learn to think Christianly, to participate in history in thoroughly Christian ways, and to value as Christians should. I would think it worthwhile if a student, when asked what he learned in college, could reply "I learned what it is to see and think and act like the human person God made me to be."

If the person, including what he becomes in this life, has an eternal destiny, then what I become in the process of education lives forever. In that sense I can take with me some of the benefits of a liberal education, while the benefits of vocational training last only for the duration of the job for which it equips me here and now. Christian liberal arts education has an eternity in view.

# 4 INTEGRATING FAITH AND LEARNING

It is not sufficient for a Christian college to identify itself simply as a liberal arts institution; it is also an extended arm of the church. We have laid aside various inadequate attempts to justify the combination. A Christian college does not exist to combine good education with a protective atmosphere, for Christians believe that the source of evil is ultimately within a man, not without. The Christian college does not exist only to offer biblical and theological studies, for these are available in other kinds of institutions, and could be offered through adjunct programs at state universities without the tremendous expense of offerings in the arts and sciences. The distinctive of the Christian college is not that it cultivates piety and religious commitment, for this could be done by church-sponsored residence houses on secular campuses. Rather the Christian college is distinctive in that the Christian faith can touch the entire range of life and learning to which a liberal education exposes students.

In principle Christian perspectives are all-redeeming and all-transforming, and it is this which gives rise to the idea of integrating faith with learning. I say "in principle" because often in practice faith and learning interact rather than integrate. Integration is an ideal never fully accomplished by anyone but God himself. Public relations material sometimes states that faith and learning are integrated on campus, as if a stroke of the pen makes it an accomplished fact, but there is many a miss and fumble and bungle between the purpose and the achievement. Interaction differs from integration. In interaction the two sit side by side in real contact with each other and engage in

47

dialog on a variety of particulars. Yet we need more than this if we are going to relate faith and learning as a coherent whole from the ground up.

Sometimes even interaction has been repressed in favor of indoctrination, as if prepackaged answers can satisfy inquiring minds. Students need rather to gain a realistic look at life and to discover for themselves the questions men confront. They need to work their way painfully through the maze of alternative ideas and arguments while finding out how the Christian faith speaks to such matters. They need a teacher as a catalyst and guide, one who has struggled and is struggling with similar questions and knows some of the pertinent materials and procedures. They need to be exposed to the frontiers of learning where problems are still not fully formulated and knowledge is exploding, and where by the very nature of things indoctrination is impossible.

Sometimes interaction between faith and learning has been at little more than a defensive level, an apologetic against challenges to the faith from the world of thought, or a Christian critique of its competitors. Apologetics undoubtedly has a place, but the Christian college has a larger and more constructive job than this. Integration is concerned not so much with attack and defense as with the positive contributions of human learning to an understanding of the faith and to the development of a Christian world-view, and with the positive contribution of the Christian faith to all the arts and sciences of man. Certainly learning has contributed from all fields to the church's understanding and propagation of its faith, from the early church to the present day, and the Christian college can contribute signally in that way. But it must also grasp what is not as often recognized, that faith affects learning far more deeply than learning affects faith.

Integration should be seen not as an achievement or a position but as an intellectual activity that goes on as long as we keep learning anything at all. We can get at it by focusing on those points of contact which faith and learning naturally have in common.

## A PERSONAL POINT OF CONTACT

The first contact is in the person of the student or teacher. Here faith and learning inevitably touch, however untheological the subject matter may be. There are some disciplines in a Christian liberal arts college to which the specific content of the Christian faith makes no evident difference. What difference does it make, for example, to mathematics? The Dutch Christian philosopher, Herman Dooyeweerd, talks about a "Christian mathematics." In actuality he is discussing the impact of the Christian faith not on the proofs and procedures of mathematics, but rather on the philosophy of mathematics, its ultimate foundations as seen from a Christian as against a non-Christian point of view, the fact that God made mathematics possible. Prior to such theological approaches to the theoretical foundations of a discipline is the attitude of the teacher or student, and this emerges as faith touches learning in his personal experience. If I were teaching symbolic logic, which is as close as a philosopher comes to mathematics, my Christianity would come through in my attitude and my intellectual integrity, rather than in the content of the course. A positive inquiring attitude and a disciplined mind would express the value I place on learning because of my Christian commitment and my theology.

A positive attitude to liberal learning is not always evident among Christians. From time to time in the history of the church as in history generally, a kind of anti-intellectualism has erupted or a cultural escapism. But the Christian faith rightly understood creates a positive attitude to liberal learning because in God's creation every area of life and learning is related to the wisdom and power of God. All truth is God's.

The same positive attitude affects more than the pursuit of truth. In his famous *City of God* Augustine proposes a Christian conception of a just society in place of Cicero's pagan view: justice is giving to each his due, including God, and that ability, like every good and perfect gift, comes from God. It therefore takes reverence and love for God to motivate man adequately toward justice. The same attitude should affect aesthetic values like beauty and creativity. All beauty is from God no matter where it is found, the artistic creativity of men is God's good gift, the potential of physical materials for being formed and fashioned into objects of art is God's doing. Some writers have even developed an aesthetic argument for the existence of God, based on the correlation between man's creative capacity in the arts and the adaptability of the world to his creativity. In God's creation every area of the liberal arts has to do with God.

Elton Trueblood has said that the Christian scholar is likely to be a better scholar for being a Christian than he would be otherwise. The comparison is not between the Christian and the non-Christian scholar, because there are other variables involved when you compare two people, but between the one individual as Christian and the same person as non-Christian. The reason, says Trueblood, is motivation, for the Christian faith is the sworn enemy of all intellectual dishonesty and shoddiness.[1] The Christian believes that in all that he does intellectually, socially or artistically, he is handling God's creation and that is sacred.

Shortly after World War II Arnold Nash wrote that one of the main tasks of the Christian scholar in higher education is to discover the meaning of Christian vocation.[2] I submit that an attitudinal contact with Christianity gives meaning to the vocation of a chemist or a sociologist, a historian or psychologist, a mathematician or an artist. The scholar's love of truth becomes an expression of his love for God, just as the citizen's love of justice in society can be an expression of his hunger and thirst for righteousness, and the artist's love for the creative and the beautiful expresses his love for the Creator.

This is where the Christian college student must begin. The first task of integration is at the personal level of attitude and motivation. In an overtly Christian college, Christian teachers dealing with Christian students have a point of appeal that is not available elsewhere. Admittedly motivating students is difficult. Adolescents have a tendency to intellectual sloppiness and their characteristic self-interestedness comes out as much in the life of the mind as anywhere. Enthusiasm for liberal learning often runs against the peer-group attitude that general educa-

---

[1] *The Idea of a College* (Harper, 1959), p. 19.
[2] *The University in the Modern World* (Macmillan, 1944), p. 292.

tion is a necessary evil to be gotten out of the way as soon and as painlessly as possible, rather than an alluring window on God's creation. It also runs against the suspicion with which many have been taught to regard the intellect, and against their cultural isolation. Yet if the highest end of man is to glorify God and to enjoy him forever, we must pursue this end here and now by exploring and enjoying the richness of his creation, and we can do so in Christian liberal arts education.

Somehow or other the student must realize that his education is a Christian vocation, his prime calling from God for these years, that his education must be an act of love, of worship, of stewardship, a wholehearted response to God. Attitude and motivation accordingly afford but a beginning; the personal contact between faith and learning should extend to disciplined scholarship and to intellectual and artistic integrity.

The college must therefore cultivate an atmosphere of Christian learning, a level of eager expectancy that is picked up by anyone who is on campus for even a short while. It must sell the idea from the point of student recruitment and admission through freshman orientation into the residence hall program, the curriculum and individual courses. The chapel program must exemplify this attitude rather than the unthinking disjunction that is all too frequent between faith and devotion on the one hand and what goes on in the classroom on the other. In campus publications, in the counseling program, a perennial salesman's job has to be done on the idea that liberal education is the Christian vocation of students as well as teachers. And required general education courses must present not narrow specializations in isolation from each other, but ideas that stretch the mind, open up historical perspective, enlarge windows on the world, and reveal the creative impact of Christian faith and thought.

The most important single factor is the teacher and his attitude to learning. By virtue of what he is his students can stand on his shoulders and peer further in their day than he did in his. From the teacher the alluring contours of a Christian mind begin to emerge.

## THE THEOLOGICAL POINT OF CONTACT

Christian theology touches the subject matter of many other disciplines. The division between disciplines is secondary to the unity of truth, and so we must avoid compartmentalizing departments. Various aspects of theology touch the arts and sciences, and two examples of this have already arisen: we have seen that the doctrines of creation and of man affect our views on education. A Christian college faculty might fruitfully work through the major topics of systematic theology, asking how each topic touches the natural sciences, the social sciences, and the humanities.

The greatest effect of Christian theology is undoubtedly in the humanities, because there we find explicit views of man and God, of morals and of life. Yet paradoxically Christians have frequently exhibited least interest here. The next greatest influence is in the social and behavioral sciences, where the nature of man undergirds his behavior and his institutions. The least far-ranging impact of Christian theology is in the natural sciences, despite the fact that more has probably been written about the relationship of Christianity to science than to other areas. Evangelicals have stressed the "how" of creation, yet the biblical teaching has more far-reaching essentials: one is in the essential character of theism as against Gnostic dualism and pantheism and naturalism. As Langdon Gilkey well shows in his *Maker of Heaven and Earth,* creation *ex nihilo* speaks to the problems of good and evil, freedom and individuality and meaning in life. Another essential is the uniqueness of man in the image of God. The effect of these items on the content of natural science is much less than their effect in the social sciences and humanities. In addition, the doctrines of sin and grace, biblical conceptions of history and of social justice and the whole range of doctrines need exploring.

If Christian theology affects other disciplines, then in the Christian college the teacher must have some understanding of theology, its biblical basis and its historical development. No matter what his teaching field, he needs to be an "avocational" student of Scripture. In the overall curriculum biblical and theological studies have an integrational role. I say "integrational" because while a college may talk about the centrality of biblical studies, in practice it can too easily compartmentalize them and leave them unrelated to psychology, art or political morality. Biblical and theological studies must be conducted not only with the academic integrity worthy of any discipline, but also with responsibility to other areas of the curriculum and with interdisciplinary dialog.

## THE INTERPRETIVE CONTACT

A third point of contact is in the interpretation of materials. "Interpretation" and "explanation" are highly ambiguous terms, for which at least three meanings are possible. One has to do with cause and effect, so that we explain a historical event or a social phenomenon by identifying its causes or effects. But *what* causes and consequences we emphasize depends not only on the data we gather, but also on the theory of historical causation with which we work. The Marxist regards economic causes as paramount and the Freudian looks for psychological causes. What about the Christian? Whatever causal explanation he offers, for all its economic and psychological ingredients, must somehow be consonant with a Christian view of man and history. Integration therefore requires attention to interpretive concepts such as historical causation and to the underlying views of man and society on which they depend.

Another possible meaning of "interpretation" has to do with conceptual relationships. The concept of revolution is tied to concepts of human rights and political authority and legitimate violence, from all of which emerge theoretical schemes that give our thinking order and unity. But just as each concept in the scheme depends on the other component concepts, so each local conceptual scheme depends on other conceptual schemes. Political theory relates to ethical theory and to religious thought and to one's view of man and the world in which he lives; they are part of a much larger world-view. The Christian needs therefore to put Christian perspectives to work in trying to understand the materials with which he may be involved.

A third possible meaning of "interpretation" has to do with the evaluation of what occurs or is reported. The positivist tried to separate fact from value; he reduced human knowledge to factual description and value judgments to purely relative emotions. As a result biologists and sociologists and others have often shied away from making value judgments about the possibility of genetic engineering or changing patterns of sexual behavior or such like. The implication is that whatever is factually possible is in principle acceptable. But the Christian cannot adopt the positivist stance. Positivism itself makes a value judgment about value judgments as compared with factual knowledge. The Christian must rather examine his values and how they bear on the materials with which he works, and must actively bring them to bear.

It is not enough to label things "right" or "wrong," "just" or "loving." Labels of this sort are person-relative and system-dependent. The word "love," for example, is used promiscuously today, but it means something different in a Christian context than in Segal's *Love Story* or in many popular lyrics. Confused values often ride piggyback on identical terms. We must teach how values are based and how value judgments are made, and we must work through the value judgments needed in our disciplines. The writing and teaching of history, for example, cannot be value-free. I think of how a British high school history text in the 1930's introduced me to the American revolution—in a footnote to Colonial history entitled "The Revolt of the American Colonies." The organization of materials and the terminology employed expressed a value judgment. Whether we speak of "revolt" or of "revolution" makes all the difference in the world to an evaluation of the facts.

In teaching, value judgments should not be moralizing tacked on at the end of a supposedly factual recital, nor should they be pontificated. Rather an evaluative process can run all the way through the structure of a course in the development of recurrent themes, in its assumptions and methods and emphases. I taught the history of philosophy for over fifteen years and learned to make and to justify my value judgments by weaving them into the structural development of the course as well as into specific lectures. It may be true that a social science does not as such make Christian value judgments, but the Christian social scientist is still not a schizophrenic. If he is a Christian, Christian value judgments somehow or other will intrude, consciously or unconsciously, into his work. It had better be conscious and well reasoned rather than unconscious and unreasoned, or else it will likely appear dishonest and be confused.

The interpretation of subject matter involves us in philosophy as well as theology, and perhaps more so. The problem of cause and effect belongs to philosophy and ideas of historical causation belong to the philosophy of history; political and ethical theories are part of philosophy as well, along with value theory as the basis for moral and aesthetic judgment. We run into philosophical problems willy-nilly.

We can conceive these relationships in terms of three concentric circles, the second of which is divided into three segments representing the natural sciences, social sciences and

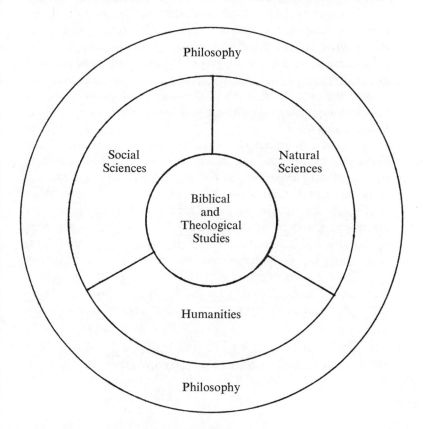

humanities. The innermost circle denotes biblical and theological studies, which are at the heart of a Christian's thinking, and the outermost circle represents philosophy. As we work from a biblical and theological perspective into the humanities and sciences we encounter problems of a foundational sort that are themselves neither theological nor scientific nor artistic, questions about causation, about the nature of moral judgment, about human knowledge generally. Theology itself poses similar questions about the logic of religious belief or the existence of God. These foundational questions are the subject matter of philosophy.

It follows that philosophy will help us to relate faith and learning at the level of foundational concepts. The biblical revelation integrates thought by providing a unifying perspective, while philosophy explores underlying problems in metaphysics (e.g. cause and effect), in epistemology (e.g. human knowledge) and in axiology (e.g. values and value judgments), and the Christian philosopher does so from a Christian perspective.[3] A Christian college must accordingly attend to such areas as philosophy of science, philosophy of the arts, ethics and political theory, philosophy of history and philosophy of education, rather than confining itself to discussions of genetics or art criticism or pedagogy without exploring their philosophical foundation.

In recent psychology, for example, the problems posed for Christians by Skinner and others are not empirical questions to be settled by experimental findings. Underlying any scientific work are epistemological questions: about the nature and limits of scientific knowledge, the use of models and so on. Behavioral conditioning may be observable in certain kinds of human conduct, but it is not therefore a sufficient cause of all a man does. Questions about the nature of man are not the same as questions about human behavior, and they cannot be answered by behavioral science alone. Yet they inevitably arise as Christians interpret the findings of contemporary behavioral science. To de-

---

[3] The relation of Christianity to philosophic inquiry is discussed more fully in my *Christian Philosophy in the Twentieth Century* (Craig Press, 1969) and *Faith Seeks Understanding* (Eerdmans, 1971).

velop Christian perspectives adequately in psychology requires that we tackle the philosophical questions.

Unfortunately the gaps between our disciplines too often prevent the benefits of interdepartmental interaction. Too often the psychologist is unacquainted with the philosophical limitations of empirical methods or with recent philosophical work on the nature of mind. And the sociologist is often a stranger to ethical theory and so a novice at arguing on other than dogmatic or utilitarian grounds. Nor do philosophers necessarily help. Too many of them are content to insulate themselves within their analyses rather than interacting with the sciences their work should affect.

Somehow this syndrome must be broken. Interdisciplinary courses are premature before the teachers involved know enough about each others' fields to construct and conduct a unified course. Time must first be found for interdisciplinary dialog among faculty. Meanwhile it would help if every student were required to take not only a general introduction to philosophy that stresses the nature of philosophical inquiry and selects from the heritage of Western thought, but also a course that bridges either outward from another discipline toward philosophy or inward from philosophy to another discipline. Philosophy of science or of mind, social ethics or aesthetics, philosophy of history or religion, of politics or law—these are the courses that address the foundational questions with which other disciplines contact philosophy. At least a requirement in these areas would help the next generation of college teachers to do what the present generation has not always been able to accomplish in interpreting scientific and scholarly findings.

## THE IDEA OF A WORLD-VIEW

The interpretation of materials introduces the final and most embracing point of contact between Christianity and human learning, the idea of an all-encompassing world and life view. The Christian faith enables us to see all things in relationship to God as their Creator, Redeemer and Lord, and from this central focus an integrating world-view emerges. The contemporary university tends to concentrate on the parts rather than the whole and to come away with a fragmented view of life that lacks overall meaning. Arnold Nash calls this tendency "intellectual polytheism,"[4] to underscore that it is as much a commitment to a world-view as is Christian theism. The influence of intellectual polytheism has been calamitous. When a multitude of studies is conducted with no interrelationships the university becomes a multiversity. In theory the university rejects attempts to teach any one conception of the world but in practice it teaches a fragmented view of life. Even to take a "neutral" position is to take some position. The world-viewish issue cannot be avoided.

More recently Robert Brombaugh, Professor of Philosophy at Yale University, stated in his Presidential Address to the Metaphysical Society of America,

> We are doing an increasingly brisk and precise job in secondary school science in demonstrating the case for a world of fact that admits no glimmer of caprice, freedom, or chance in its causal order. We are doing an increasingly more crucial job of awakening a sense of responsibility in our students. Sometimes they feel this responsibility toward society, sometimes toward their own authenticity. But we are doing nothing at all to explain this schizophrenic change in the conception of reality that varies with each move between classrooms. We are upset by the attempts of our students to retain some intellectual integrity: by apathy, by indiscriminate activism, by distrust of an intelligence and authority that has set them a puzzle they must solve, with pieces that cannot be fitted together into any solution.[5]

It is a sad paradox that on the one hand the scientific outlook declares that nature is intelligible and rationally ordered in both its macroscopic and its microscopic aspects, and on the other hand the existentialist tells us that life is devoid of any intrinsic meaning and intelligible order at all. This is a schizophrenic day that desperately needs an integrated understanding, a worldview that can stick fragmented pieces together. The Christian is

---

[4] *The University and the Modern World,* pp. 258ff.
[5] "Applied Metaphysics: Truth and Passing Time," *Review of Metaphysics,* XIX (1966), 650f.

obliged to develop a Christian world-view, believing as he does that the Christian message heals.

But what do we mean by a world-view, a *Weltanschauung?* The notion needs unpacking, and I suggest four characteristics.[6]

The first and most obvious is that a world-view is holistic or integrational. It sees things not just as parts but also as a whole. It is a systematic understanding and appraisal of life, and none of the academic disciplines is exempted from contact with it.

Second, a world-view is exploratory, not a closed system worked out once and for all but an endless undertaking that is still but the vision of a possibility, an unfinished symphony barely begun. It explores the creative and redemptive impact of the Christian revelation on every dimension of thought and life, and it remains open-ended because the task is so vast that to complete it would require the omniscience of God. To begin requires an intelligent understanding of the Christian revelation, and from this first glimpse of truth as a whole endless inquiry grows. We should not expect the Christian college to propound a definite and complete Christian view of things, for it is premature to finalize all the details of a Christian view of this, that or anything. Christian perspectives are possible, but not a complete and definitive system. Who are we bungling, stuttering creatures to exhaust any subject? Now we see through a glass darkly; we know in part.

Third, a Christian world-view is likely to be pluralistic. If it is an open-ended exploration you cannot expect complete unanimity—not that there is much virtue in human unanimity anyway. Even within a particular Christian tradition, say the Reformed, there should be room for pluralism in the development of various perspectives each equally loyal to Reformed theology. Historic Christianity taken as a whole has been even more pluralistic. Diversity exists not only because of theological differences but also because we explore Christian perspectives on the world of thought at different points and by different paths

---

[6] They are discussed more fully in relation to the idea of a Christian philosophy in chap. 1 of my *Christian Philosophy in the Twentieth Century.*

and with different concerns and backgrounds. This is why academic freedom and intellectual honesty are so essential.

Fourth, a world-view is confessional or perspectival. We need not proceed deductively from universal and necessary truths, from either axioms or scientifically demonstrable propositions, so I prefer not to call the starting point "presuppositions." Rather we start with a confession of faith, with an admixture of beliefs and attitudes and values. Good and sufficient reason may be given for what we believe, but ours is still a confessional stance and from the perspective of this confession we look at life. We see things from a Christian point of view.

A perspectival world and life view is not the same as a theology: Christian theology is a study of the perspective itself as disclosed by the biblical revelation. It looks within, whereas a Christian world-view looks without, at life and thought in other departments and disciplines, in order to see these other things from the standpoint of revelation and as an interrelated whole. Integration is ultimately concerned to see things whole from a Christian perspective, to penetrate thought with that perspective, to think Christianly.

The four characteristics of a world-view, then, are that it is (1) holistic, (2) exploratory, (3) pluralistic and (4) perspectival, and the four points of contact I have suggested between faith and learning are (1) the personal, (2) the theological, (3) the interpretive and (4) the world-viewish.

## A HISTORICAL STARTING POINT

For centuries Christians have explored these points of contact, and that fact suggests that one readily available method of exhibiting interrelationships and provoking integration is the historical. What does the history of science or of art or of philosophy show of the creative and redemptive impact of Christian beliefs and values on human culture? What about the influence of Christianity on eighteenth-century social history in England? What about the influence of the religious changes in the eighteenth and nineteenth centuries on painting? What about the origins of modern science?

With regard to the last of these examples, the philosopher and scientist A. N. Whitehead suggests that early modern science developed because of the encouragement given to it in the religious atmosphere of the Middle Ages. This thesis has been challenged, but if it is not overstated I think it can be substantiated. The atmosphere of the Middle Ages was pervaded by the theistic conviction that because God is the rational and wise Creator, his handiwork is therefore intelligible to beings in God's image. This theistic atmosphere which expected the natural order to be amenable to rational inquiry was the natural birthplace of scientific inquiry. Forty years ago, the British philosopher Michael Foster published a series of articles arguing that the Greek conception that eternal forms determine the course of nature led the ancients to rationalistic speculations about nature rather than to empirical observation, until the theistic insistence prevailed in science as in theology that nature is contingent on God. There is no intrinsic necessity that it exist or that it be the way it is. If it is God's creation, it is contingent on God, and the scientist can no longer operate on an a priori basis but must be more empirical if he is to find out how nature does in fact behave. The result, according to Foster, was the growth of Renaissance science.[7]

The historical method has considerable merit in the humanities. In introducing students to philosophy, one obvious way to expose the effect of Christian perspectives is to include readings from first-rate philosophers of the past who were themselves Christian theists. That is usually far more effective than a teacher's own half-baked, underdeveloped notions. One might include Christian philosophers of different sorts: Augustine's Christianization of Cicero; Aquinas' use of Aristotelian ideas; Descartes, Leibniz, Locke and Berkeley and their attempts to justify and limit human reason in dependence on God, while avoiding the dangers inherent in the current mechanistic view of nature and of man; Kierkegaard's criticism of Enlightenment epistemology and ethics. Christian philosophers as different as

---

[7] A. N. Whitehead, *Science and the Modern World* (Mentor Books, 1948), p. 14; M. B. Foster in *Mind*, XLIII (1934), 446; XLIV (1935), 439; XLV (1936), 1.

these reflect the pluralism within a Christian world-view, yet they share the common belief that God created all things and that man is uniquely in God's image, and they develop the creative impact of these ideas on the problems they wrestled with and in the positions they set forth.

Be it the history of science or of philosophy or of art or whatever, we have available historical samples of faith in creative contact with learning, contacts of the kinds we have called personal and theological and interpretive and world-viewish.

# 5 EXPERIENCE IS NOT ENOUGH

We have seen that the value of a liberal education is rooted in Christian theology (Chap. 2), that the concept of a liberal education depends on the nature of man (Chap. 3), and that Christian higher education depends on biblical as well as creational sources of knowledge. Now we must take account of the nature of knowledge itself. In recent years the empiricist theory that knowledge is basically experience has captured a wide popular following, despite the philosophical criticism to which it has been exposed. In this chapter we shall argue that the limitations of empiricism as a theory of knowledge indicate that experience is not enough for an education. First, some comments on "experience," then two arguments in support of my thesis, and finally something about the positive contributions of experience to education.

## WHAT IS EXPERIENCE?

The term "experience" is like a can of worms: you cannot be sure what it contains until you unpack it. For years the emphasis was on scientific experience with its objective and repeatable data. That created problems, first by limiting the range of admissible experience to what is scientifically observable, second by overgeneralizing from a limited range of data, and third by forgetting that observations are never wholly independent of the working hypotheses of the scientist. Philosophers from Hume to Russell and Wittgenstein have pressed these limitations on scientific empiricism, and recent philosophy of science points out that scientific observations are theory-dependent. Science itself is thus not purely empirical, and experience

63

is not enough even for science. We therefore ask how it can be enough for education.

Nowadays less emphasis is placed in education on the sufficiency of scientific experience. The term "experience" is often used instead in the pragmatist sense of a process of trial and error whereby we learn to handle particular problems. America has always had a pragmatic temperament, but ours in particular is a "how to do it" age. We are treated to a rash of "how to do it" books about everything from Christian living to organic gardening. Many of them offer easy formulae without any theoretical basis, formulae based on someone's personal experience that may or may not be generalizable for others. In education, ours is an age of *ad hoc* learning, a potpourri of piecemeal "how to do it" courses that hold immediate interest or have immediate use in some current situation, rather than of systematic approaches that explore historical and theoretical foundations and have a myriad of still unseen applications.

The *ad hoc* approach may be called "situational education." But situational education is objectionable in the same ways as situational ethics, for what works in one situation at one time may or may not work in another situation at another time. What is practical here today may not be as practical elsewhere. The relevance of today is the irrelevance of tomorrow. Everything becomes relative; the practical without firm theoretical principle is a "blind leader of the blind." If the practical and situational emphasis is not to become another relativism, it needs checks and balances. It needs (as we saw in Chaps. 1 and 3) the guidance of a historical perspective and of theoretical concepts that adequately interpret the present and past alike, and so enable us to anticipate the future. It needs lasting values and lasting truth. Ideas are not true because they are practical, although they may prove practical because they are true. Our first priority must be the quest for unchanging truth, not for practical experience.

Relevance is in demand. In addition to stressing the practical it calls for immediate and firsthand experiences. But how can we direct such experiences instead of being directed by them, and how can we evaluate what we feel, without some basis for judgment and without understanding the processes that shape our present as they shaped the past? The first prerequisite for relevance is a sense of history and the second a basis of evaluation, for without them experience is uninformed and ill-directed, wavering amid the onslaught of conflicting whims and pressures. Experience alone is not enough.

It is not enough that we concentrate in education on scientific facts, for as soon as we generalize or explain or even record our observations, as selective and interpretive as human perception is, we discover that experience is not enough. Nor is the important thing that we concentrate on the practical, for practice without theory becomes a bungling process of trial and error; nor that we stress the present relevance of what we do, for all our todays are gone tomorrow. Experience changes; it is not self-interpreting; it is not therefore enough. We must also understand truth that does not change and grasp the relation of true theory to effective practice, of understanding to experience, and of the past to the present and future.

Today the term "experience" has yet another meaning, a neo-Romanticist emphasis on affective rather than cognitive states, sometimes on the aesthetic rather than the intellectual. It is evident in the renewal of simple folk arts, in artificially expanded sense awareness, in the rediscovery of mystical religion. The stress is on pervasive and immediate feelings rather than on analyzing, interpreting and evaluating what we experience. The neo-Romanticist influence in education must be watched closely. There is nothing either morally bad or unworthy of man in heightened feelings *per se*. There is nothing wrong and nothing degrading in walking barefoot in the park and feeling the grass between my toes, nor in men's hair as well as women's blowing in the breeze, nor in wildly colored clothes, nor in discovering physical sensations and emotive responses I never knew existed. Nor is there anything wrong with laboratory experience in the ghetto, nor with giving P.E. credit for stress programs, nor with opportunities for artistic expression. The question is not whether affective experience is to be discouraged but whether unexamined experience is enough, whether it be unexamined ghetto experience or unexamined physical stress or the unexamined activity of taking photographs or fashioning free-form sculptures. Experience may provide effective training, it may be an eye-opener, it may be exciting and enriching, it may attract student interest and increase enrollments. But is it by itself education?

My point is that in whichever sense we speak of "experience" the same conclusion follows. Neither scientific experience, nor the relevance of a situational approach, nor affective experience is enough for the purposes of education.

## TWO ARGUMENTS

To make the case as obvious as possible, I present two simple syllogisms.

*Syllogism #1:*
> Experience alone is not understanding.
> Education seeks understanding.
> Therefore experience alone is not education.

*The first premise,* "experience alone is not understanding," has a familiar ring to anyone acquainted with the history of philosophy, for Plato went into great detail in his *Theaetetus* to show that this is so. Perception is not knowledge, he argued, for perceptual experience varies with the observer's physical and psychological condition. It makes a difference whether we are tired or fresh, attentive or confused, close to or distant from an object, in front of it or beside it. A coin, for instance, is seen as circular, elliptical or a straight line, depending on the vantage point of the observer. A dog hears a whistle pitched too high for the human ear. It also makes a difference when objects of experience change and, as Plato pointed out, all physical things change in some way. The tree outside my window looks different in October than in December and again in April or May. People change, and so do political structures and social mores. We cannot base unchanging knowledge on changing experience of changing things. Experience yields none of the lasting truth that understanding seeks.

Such is Plato's argument. As a rationalist he may have underestimated the contribution of experience to understanding, but he is nonetheless correct about the changeableness and relativity of human experience. I therefore moderate his conclusion by adding the word "alone," and affirm that experience *alone* is not enough.

Another classic problem was exhibited by David Hume. Experience is always limited in scope: we have our present experience, but we do not now experience the past in the same way we did, nor do we yet experience the future. How can we know what lies beyond our present experience? Yet we need to if we are to learn from the past and plan for the future. And we claim to know more than our present experience every time we generalize. Some scientific theories are of this sort, generalizations based on present and past experience and applicable to future experience. In fact the predictive power of a scientific theory is one of its principal virtues. Yet Hume pointed out that generalizations can be drawn from present experience only by assuming the uniformity of nature. But that is the very point at stake, namely that the future is like the present and the past. It seems, then, that empirical generalizations are without logical grounds: they rest on generalizations about uniformity that experience itself can never finally establish. However we broaden our observations and enrich our sensitivities, the same problem persists. Experience alone is not enough to support the generalized understanding that education seeks.

A third problem, posed by Immanuel Kant, is of particular interest to Christians. Experience is not self-interpreting. The word "interpretation" is another can of worms: as we noted in the last chapter it can mean (a) the discovery of causes and consequences, (b) exploring conceptual relations or (c) making value judgments. But whichever way we take it, we have to introduce assumptions that experience alone cannot establish. In the case of (a) we introduce the idea of cause and effect; in regard to (b) we employ various kinds of logical relationship; in (c) we need the idea of right and wrong or good and bad. None of these assumptions, Kant argued, is derived from experience: they are rather the presuppositions of intelligible experience. Kant regarded them as universal and necessary. I am inclined to regard them more as part of an underlying world-view that we bring to experience. Even then interpretation depends on presuppositions, and if they vary from one world-view to another, our interpretations will too.

The Christian educator should realize that the presuppositions a man brings to his experience, be they Christian or non-Christian, shape his understanding. Experience is not self-interpreting. For example, the French Catholic existentialist Gabriel Marcel and the French atheistic existentialist Jean-Paul Sartre interpret interpersonal relationships very differently. In his play *A Man of God,* Marcel finds a glimmer of faith and love and hope where Sartre in *No Exit* finds only negation and absurdity. Again, the student radical who followed Marcuse in tracing his unhappy experience to modern economic structures adopted Marcuse's neo-Marxist presuppositions about economic causation in history.

My point is that if understanding seeks unchanging truth that covers a variety of changing moods and experiences (Plato's problem), if understanding requires generalization beyond our present experience (Hume's problem), if understanding involves interpretation and evaluation (Kant's problem), then experience alone is not the same as understanding and our first premise is established.

*The second premise* is that education seeks understanding or, to be more precise, the goals of liberal education center on human understanding and appreciation. Here again we must distinguish liberal education from its neighbors. It is not synonymous with training, which develops skills; nor is it the same as indoctrination, which imposes information with a view to unquestioning assent. Training and indoctrination seek to determine student behavior, but liberal education prepares for the wise exercise of freedom through the development of the understanding. Nor is liberal education to be equated with a general education that ensures breadth. General education tries to overcome the limited scope of ordinary experience and knowledge, but liberal education is concerned not only with broad scope but also with seeing things as an interrelated whole, therefore with understanding truth and value, with presuppositions that help us interpret experience and make reasonable value judgments. My point is that by definition if we are engaged in liberal education we have to do with the development of understanding, and our second premise is established.

*The conclusion* follows: if experience alone is not understanding and if education seeks understanding, then experience alone is not enough for education.

*Syllogism #2:*

> Experience is primarily affective.
> Education is not primarily affective but has to do with the whole person.
> Therefore experience alone is not enough for an education.

*The first premise* is self-evident if by experience we mean today's neo-Romanticist attention to feeling and sensation. But it is also true of experience generally, for the awarenesses and feelings that comprise experience become informative and cognitive only as we arrest them in our attention, reflect upon them, describe and generalize, interpret and evaluate. Raw, unexamined experience is not primarily cognitive but affective: it elicits concern, it excites and confuses, it pleases and it pains, it provokes reaction.

Education, on the other hand, is not concerned with raw, unprocessed experience, but with the cognitive as well as the affective states, indeed with developing the whole person. This is the cliché to which we at least pay lip service. Our *second premise* therefore calls attention to the nature of persons, and here Christian perspectives are of particular importance.

As we saw in Chapter 3, from a Christian standpoint the rationalist conception of man that came down from Plato and Aristotle and the Roman Stoics to the Enlightenment will not do. Augustine saw through it, as did Pascal and Kierkegaard and Reinhold Niebuhr and Herman Dooyeweerd. This is not to say that man is *not* a rational being: anti-intellectualism, whether in Romanticism or in pietism, finds no support in the biblical doctrine of man. But it is to say that human personality is significantly more complex than Plato or Cicero or Descartes or John Locke purports. Augustine in his *City of God* took Cicero to task for supposing that reason alone can always tell us what is right, and for expecting men to live and act under the rule of reason. A man is what he is and acts as he does by virtue of what he supremely loves. Pascal's famous dictum is along similar lines, that the heart (which the Bible treats not as the emotions but as the inner root of the whole person) has reasons that the intellect alone does not know. And Kierkegaard draws attention to passion (by which he means not just feeling but whole-person involvement) and to subjecthood (a better rendering than the usual "subjectivity") in order to get away from the narrow rationalism of a Descartes or Hegel. We live and think, we moralize and socialize, we encounter the truth and stand before God in sin and grace, as whole persons.

But man is still a rational being, not in the sense of calculative reasoning or that logical certainty is readily available or that man can rule and be ruled by what he knows, but in a richer sense that speaks to our intellectual curiosity and capacity for understanding. It implies that education, concerned as it is with developing the whole person, must further man's quest for intelligible meaning; it will stretch the mind, inform the understanding, and teach people to think logically and to detect and examine presuppositions. Christian education must do all of this in the light of Scripture, for propositional revelation as well as education is addressed to men as rational beings.

In the second place, we are valuing beings who pursue moral and social and aesthetic and intellectual ideals, and Christian liberal arts education is concerned with student values. From the time of David Hume through the Romanticist and the positivist eras into the present day there has been a tendency to reduce value to feeling, so that to say I value honesty means that it pleases me and to say that stealing is wrong means it pains me. The Romanticists and their present-day stepchildren give this an aesthetic twist, so that stealing becomes obscene, and honesty is "beautiful." Aesthetic criteria such as inner harmony are interpreted as enriched feelings and emotional fulfilment, and are converted into criteria for goodness and truth. But as we indicated previously, the emotivist theory of value fails. It violates the very nature of man, for love (to take another example) is not just an emotive state, it involves my understanding of the person I adore, it involves openness, moral obligation and a free and full commitment to give what I am and have.

Underlying both the emotivist and the rationalist fallacies is an outmoded faculty psychology that divided man into intellect, emotion and will. As a result one or another of these faculties vies for supremacy: we are supposed to be either rationalists *or* emotivists *or* voluntarists. In our day of more holistic personality theory, the mistake is evident: reason is an activity, not a faculty or an element in man but an activity of the whole person whose "reasons" include his values and purposes and life-commitments as well as his arguments and scientific evidence. Feeling is a person's conscious reaction that can never be filtered out from either his reasoning or his valuing. The cognitive and the affective are inseparably united in the structural unity of the whole person. So we excite to ideas, we have heated arguments, and we give reasons for feeling (*sic!*) the way we do about our wives, about stealing, about Christian higher education, and about Wordsworth's daffodils.

But if man is a valuing being and education has to do with the whole person, then we should be concerned with the transmission and formation of values. If personality is value-oriented and there are no value-free persons, then an education that concerns itself with whole persons cannot escape responsibility in the classroom and outside for student values. We make value judgments by our curricular and pedagogical decisions as well as by the explicit consideration of moral and social and aesthetic questions in the classroom and by the rules that structure campus life. The student must learn to scrutinize his values, not just to enjoy his feelings, not just to conform. He must be prepared to modify his values, and he must learn that valuing commits him to action. Even withdrawal from cultural involvement is an action embodying values.

In the third place, then, man is not only a rational and a valuing being but also a historical agent who acts. He has a past and a future that is both individual and societal, and he participates in shaping his future, both individual and societal. If education has to do with the whole person, it is mandatory that the student gain a sense of his history, that he identify with his past and understand the influences from the past that set parameters for his future, that he learn to make judgments, moral and otherwise, about the society of which he is part. For unless he gains this kind of liberal education he will stumble headlong into the future like a blundering bull in the proverbial china shop, with tragic consequences for himself and his family and for both church and society.

Education has to do with the whole person, then, and since experience is primarily affective, experience alone is not enough. Our second syllogism is complete. Not everything that glitters is gold: not every experience of worth, nor every experience put together, is enough for an education.

## EXPERIENCE AS EDUCATIONAL

In God's world, the Christian should obviously value experience and feeling and emotion as well as understanding. Learning should touch the real issues we experience rather than detach itself like a remote game of chess. My proposal is simply that experience can be education*al* even if by itself it is not education. Experience and education are still related: even though experience sometimes plays the chauvinist husband and tries to run Frau Education, it is in reality more like the proverbial mother-in-law. That is, she constantly intrudes on education's life; sometimes she tries to dominate, sometimes she provokes and irritates, but always she offers valuable material for thought and she remains much loved. Education can never push experience wholly out of her life; nor should she, for they are members of the same family.

The relationship is of course based on the fact that both can contribute to persons. In relation to education, experience can contribute at least three things: it motivates by capturing interest and attention, it illuminates by providing points of reference in the lived-world, and it provides raw material for the processes of interpretation of which we spoke earlier. The experience of living in the ghetto illustrates all three functions: it can be fascinating enough to interest the student in a serious study of urban problems; the firsthand encounter will make generalized and theoretical material seem concrete and realistic; and for a long time thereafter the perplexities and ambiguities of the situation will cry out for explanation and resolution.

During the latter part of the Vietnam conflict, I offered a course called "The Morality of War." Student feelings ran high and provided motivation; current events and the experience of frustration and ambiguity illuminated the historical and philosophical materials under study. More important, a careful examination of the historical development of pacifism and the just war theory and a discussion of ethical, political and legal philosophy provided a sense of history and a theoretical basis for interpreting and evaluating current events reasonably rather than just "sounding off" about them. In that context, experience was educational.

But unexamined experience—what we have variously called "experience alone" and "raw experience"—is not enough, for it is not fully enough human. It must be humanized if it is to be educational, so what has been said about the nature of persons will again help us.

Man is a rational being, a valuing being and a historical agent. In the first place, then, the *experience of rational activity* can be educational. As a philosophy teacher I have to ask what experiences could contribute significantly to philosophical education. Careful consideration of the moral questions posed by war could well do so, but not just the physical and emotional stress of going to war or of resisting it unanalytically and without theoretical basis. I do not think that a student's reflections on his experience in physical stress programs merit either philosophy or psychology credit: philosophy and psychology should be far more scientific than that. A European travel program would be enriching in many ways, but seeing the carved figure of St. Anselm outside Canterbury Cathedral contributes little to my understanding or appreciation of his ontological argument and visiting the Sorbonne does not itself enable me to wrestle more effectively with Bergson or Sartre. Of course it would help to discuss their thinking with them at length but then, granted the possibility of resuscitation, it would be a lot easier and cheaper to fly them over here than for a crowd of us to go over there. Plainly, the experience of philosophical reasoning that contributes to philosophical education can be secured as effectively on campus as off. The educational value of European travel programs is more in fields like history and art than in philosophy.

Old ways of teaching did not always secure it. To lecture and examine over three or four classical positions on each of eight or nine classical problems, along with two or three classical arguments for each of the three or four classical positions about eight or nine classical problems may produce only a boring recital of annotated grocery lists. Essential to philosophical education is the experience of wrestling for oneself with problems and arguments and positions. Papers and discussions accordingly serve in philosophy as a ghetto experience might in sociology or a laboratory experience in the teaching of science; and this says something about the maximum size of philosophy classes. But papers and discussions without sufficient historical and theoretical and logical input and without painstaking criticism, while quite an experience, easily deteriorate into a trivial parading of ignorance. Experience alone is not education; to be educational it must involve informed and self-critical rational activity. As Kant reminded us, understanding requires both empirical and rational input.

In the second place, the *experience of making reasonable value judgments* can be educational, for it contributes to the development of man as a valuing being. Here again we must remember that values are not just feelings. A value judgment is the application to an individual case of aesthetic or moral or political or religious principles. The experience must therefore involve the formulation as well as the application of such principles, not in an emotionless fashion, but with sufficient detachment to be able to appraise the way we feel as well as to appraise the principles and cases in question. Sometimes our feelings will have to be brought into line with our value judgments, for feeling must ultimately conform to the truth rather than the truth conforming to however we may feel.

One art teacher I know complains that his students cannot verbalize why they feel as they do about art works, let alone formulate principles of aesthetic judgment on which to base their art criticism. To the extent that a student cannot think his way into such matters (not necessarily "through" them), he is not educated in art, but only trained. His experience is not educational unless he learns how to make defensible value judgments.

This suggests that the educational value of living in the ghetto lies not just in getting the "feel" of urban and minority problems, but rather in the experience of making well-informed and reasoned value judgments. It is not enough that the student says what he personally thinks and feels about school busing, an assignment that can engender triviality and relativism, but that he explore the viability of alternative evaluations in relation not only to the observable facts but also to the assumptions various social scientists and ethicists and theologians make about human nature and behavior. The positivist social scientist will not like this, but the Christian should by now have paid his parting compliments to positivism and come to see the impact of theological and ethical and methodological assumptions on both thought and behavior. Christian education requires that the student gain experience in detecting assumptions, in clarifying his own presuppositions, and in making his own value judgments accordingly. Too easily "field experience" can forget what should have been done in "theoretical" courses, and become entirely pragmatic.

In the third place, educational experience must be *historical experience,* for man is a historical agent. This does not mean cramming endless facts about the past but rather reliving the past empathetically so as to understand the present and participate in shaping hypothetical directions for the future.

Travel experience does not automatically guarantee this sense of history and of cultural and social involvement. The ex-G.I. who refers to ancient ruins in Italy as old rocks about which he could not care less, had travel experience but no historical experience. He gave no evidence of the educated person's understanding and appreciation of the Roman heritage in law and politics and art symbolized by "old rocks," a heritage that has shaped our present and influenced the contours of a future to which we now have the responsibility of giving specific shape. Travel experience needs input concerning political and economic and artistic and religious history if it is to be of educational worth. Experience alone is not enough.

Similar observations might be made about work-study programs and extracurricular activities. To be educational they must be conducted under the scrutiny of appropriate disciplines and with the input of theoretical and valuational and historical considerations. It is counter-productive educationally to sponsor activities, even Christian service activities, in which the student relapses into unreflective ways, or reflects without the scrutiny of a properly equipped mentor. What science teacher would dream, except in his wildest nightmares, of turning students loose in the laboratory without adequate preparation and without the collateral benefits of more theoretical and perhaps historical approaches to phenomena?

Liberal education develops the man. It is an open invitation to join the human race. Christian liberal arts education is an invitation to become increasingly a Christian man. But neither the excitement of traveling in Europe, nor the trauma of living in a ghetto, nor simply looking at paintings or making them, nor unexamined religious experience and service activities can develop the whole man, for experience is primarily affective and man is far more. Experience must be humanized if it is to be educational; to be humanized it must be educated. In the final analysis that is why raw experience is not enough; uneducated experience cannot educate.

# 6 ACADEMIC FREEDOM

On the surface at least, the Christian liberal arts college faces a dilemma. On the one hand, liberal education requires that we think critically about our heritage of faith and culture and wrestle honestly with the problems men in general and Christians in particular face in today's world. This requires freedom of inquiry for both teacher and student. On the other hand, Christian education implies commitment to the Word of God and responsibility to the church constituency a college serves. Liberty without loyalty is not Christian, but loyalty without the liberty to think for oneself is not education.

It is also true that education is impossible without loyalty to truth and intellectual honesty, and that a man without loyalties outside himself has not yet joined the human race; likewise that loyalty without liberty is not Christian but legalistic. The attempt to integrate faith and learning and to see things from a confessional perspective is, after all, an attempt to unite loyalty with liberty in Christian education.

In this chapter I want to discuss (1) why academic freedom is important in the Christian college, (2) how it may be conceived, and (3) some criticisms it meets.

## IMPORTANCE

Academic freedom is essential to the academic task. Liberal education means the stretching of minds and imaginations, the unceasing stimulus to honest inquiry, the appropriation of a cultural heritage, the transmission of ideas and values, an exposure to the frontiers of learning. By definition it requires freedom to grow, to gain stimulation and to give it, freedom to meet great minds of the past and present, to interact rigorously with their ideas and weigh their values, freedom to explore new horizons and press back the frontiers of learning—in a word, it means academic freedom.

The Germans had two words: *Lehrfreiheit,* the freedom to teach, and *Lernfreiheit,* the freedom to learn. The sort of neutrality they intended by these terms may be undesirable for both educational and religious reasons and impossible psychologically. But they serve to point up two sides to academic freedom: the faculty side and the student side. Both are of concern in liberal education, and together they amount to the freedom of a college really to be an educational institution rather than an indoctrination center or a political tool.

Further, academic freedom is essential for theological reasons. Man is not an automaton but a free agent created in God's image. If we produce stereotypes cut from the same pattern, if we repress individuality, we sin against both God and man, for individuals do not exist for individualism's sake but to live in communion with God and community with men.

But freedom is essential to faith. Freedom of thought is the freedom of the individual to think for himself with the faith he has and the beliefs and values to which he is committed. In this sense neither faith nor intellect can be forced but *must* be free, full and wholehearted, or else one does not really believe and does not think. Richard Hofstadter observes that in the Reformation period, "pious. men saw that forced acceptance of a faith would not be sincere, that instead of saving souls it created hypocrites."[1]

Academic freedom is the recognition that faith and intellect, like love, cannot be forced and must not be, if each is to play its part in relation to the other. I suspect that a considerable amount of student cynicism and scepticism can be traced to attempts to dogmatically impose a faith rather than presenting it graciously and reasonably, and to the practice of pontificating "answers" rather than assisting students in grappling with

---

[1] R. Hofstadter and W. P. Metzger, *The Development of Academic Freedom in the United States* (Columbia Univ. Press, 1955), p. 65.

issues for themselves in the light of their heritage of Christian faith and thought. We can get so busy taking the motes of immaturity out of students' eyes that we forget the beams of finiteness, fallibility and inflexibility in our own eyes.

While Scripture is our final rule of faith and practice, not all the truth about everything is fully revealed therein. If that were so we would need no natural or social sciences, no humanities and no theology—just biblical exegesis. Rather, the eternal Logos has left his imprint on nature and man and history, and the truth discovered therein is God's truth too. We approach it with reverence and humility, modest and tentative in our pronouncements. If all truth is God's truth, we must be free to explore it. If it all ultimately fits into a coherent whole, then our task is to interpret it as such by developing Christian perspectives in the natural and social sciences and the humanities, so as to structure a Christian world-view that exhibits plainly the principle that truth is one and all truth is God's. This requires open eyes and open doors on the world, not blinkers and cloisters and defensiveness about the problems.

The fact is that faith liberates rather than enslaves the mind. It helps me understand myself and my world, it creates a positive attitude to learning. Christian liberty is neither irresponsible license nor repressive bondage, and academic freedom in the Christian college must rest on this realization.

According to Russell Kirk, the medieval universities enjoyed academic freedom not despite but because of the framework of Christian belief in which they operated. Insofar as their scholars were Christian, this framework did not restrain them. Rather it protected their dialog, it guaranteed them liberty to pursue the truth in detail and in totality and to lead their students into the same enterprise of committed scholarship.

> The teacher was a servant of God wholly, and of God only. His freedom was sanctioned by an authority more than human. Now and then that freedom was violated . . . yet it scarcely occurred to anyone to attempt to regulate or to suppress the freedom of the Academic: it was regarded almost as a part of the natural and unalterable order of things.

In medieval times, it was precisely their Christian framework that gave masters and students this high confidence. Far from repressing free discussion, this framework encouraged disputation of a heated intensity almost unknown in universities nowadays. . . . They were free from a stifling internal conformity, because the whole purpose of the universities was the search after an enduring truth, beside which wordly aggrandizement was as nothing. They were free because they agreed on this one thing, if on nothing else, that the fear of God is the beginning of wisdom.[2]

Finally, academic freedom is essential to the self-scrutiny and improvement of any society. Socrates and Plato are classic examples in their struggle with the Sophists for the survival of Athenian culture. As we read Plato's dialogs, we recognize with a smile that portrait of the teacher as a skillful midwife and the experience of students who feel the birth-pangs that climax intellectual gestation. As we survey Plato's own intellectual development and examine the educational philosophy and program he presents in the *Republic,* we are impressed with his concern for society, with his emphasis on unchanging values, with his integration of the curriculum around the disciplined mind, with his emphasis on critical thinking. We note the diversity of viewpoints discussed, the lack not only of unanimity but also of dogmatic indoctrination. Admittedly he censored some of the literature of his day because it detracted from intellectual and moral growth. But we admire his relentless quest for clarity of understanding, his endless self-scrutiny, and the courageous intellectual honesty that led Socrates to lose his life and forced Plato to change his mind. The Socratic method presupposes freedom to pursue the truth even in a community that is unaccustomed to thinking and unfavorably disposed to penetrating inquiry. Socrates embarrassed and antagonized his constituencies, perhaps unnecessarily; he was accused of corrupting his students, the youth of Athens, in the final analysis because his supreme loyalty was to eternal truth rather than human opinion, and this loyalty could not be

---

[2] Russell Kirk, *Academic Freedom* (Regnery, 1955), p. 18.

swayed by the fears and psychological insecurities of others, and would not be trampled by political pressure. His motivation was not that of the Sophist libertines, but that of a loyal and responsible citizen, utterly convinced that what he did was for the common good and in the highest interests of society.

The point is that liberal education and the freedom it requires can provide the basis for an informed and responsible criticism of society. If colleges are to provide leadership, then embryonic leaders must try their wings even if first attempts fail. What better way is there to criticize and improve on the past and present than to examine it in the light of the best learning available? How else can men who are historical beings hope to transcend the past more creatively in the future?

It is likewise important to the ongoing history of the church, for its vigor in meeting new challenges and its creativity in relating unchanging truth to changing situations, that it expose itself to possible criticism based on responsible learning. It is not by accident that freedom of conscience is part of the Reformation heritage. The early leaders of the Reformation—Wycliffe, Huss and Luther—were university men and their opposition to Rome developed because they refused to think in ruts worn by tradition, superstition and ignorance. Wycliffe was stoutly defended by Oxford University against pope and bishop, and it took the combined force of church and crown to suppress his voice. Religious liberty and academic freedom went hand in hand, insisting on the right to examine the cherished and to improve on the past. Not only reformers were repressed. Aristotle and Aquinas had been banned at Paris; later, elsewhere, Descartes, Newton and Locke shared the same fate. And remember Galileo. But truth will win out. It cannot be suppressed; for in the final analysis all truth is God's.

We sadly err if we repeat the errors of the past, whether in excising twentieth-century Aristotles from the curriculum, or in seeking to silence our Galileos or Wycliffes. This is no way to face problems: it is dishonest. There is no effective alternative to academic freedom. The Christian college must provide the opportunity and the atmosphere for an open discussion of new ideas and significant issues. Hackneyed clichés and parroted answers smack more of indoctrination than education. There is no substitute for the hard work of thinking and no escape from the ever present possibility of misunderstanding.

The evangelical theologian G. C. Berkouwer states it plainly:

> An honesty which has a candid eye open to the problems of the day is basically Christian and belongs to our Christian responsibilities. If we were to renege on this Christian responsibility, we would confine Christian life to a ghetto of irrelevancy and powerlessness.[3]

To deny academic freedom is historical suicide. Rather than confirming men in the truth it will drive them from it. Rather than cherishing orthodoxy it will render it suspect to every inquiring mind. Rather than developing the intellectual resources essential to Christian thought and action it will stifle them. Rather than launching a strategic offensive into the citadels of secularism it will incarcerate us in the ill-equipped and outdated strongholds of past wars. The Church Militant cannot retreat; but to advance means facing problems squarely, entertaining new ideas, admitting and correcting mistakes. Truth is not yet fully known; every academic discipline is subject to change, correction and expansion—even theology. Students must know this and must be taught to think for themselves. On its academic front, then, the effectiveness of the Church Militant requires academic freedom.

The Christian college is a uniquely American institution, and the history of academic freedom within its halls is therefore a chapter in the history of American Christianity. Of particular importance is the rise of theological liberalism with its repudiation of biblical authority. It is little wonder that as liberal forces engulfed church-related institutions, conservatives became suspicious of the treachery that turns liberty into license. Yet it is unfortunate that in repudiating the one extreme of license, they have sometimes tended to the other extreme of legalism and become suspicious even of that academic integrity

---

[3] *Christianity Today,* August 2, 1963, p. 48.

and freedom which is an expression of Christian honesty and liberty.

Academic freedom, in other words, is a necessity, not a luxury. It is of the essence both of Christianity and of learning, and must be so defined and practiced. It is of the essence of Christianity because true freedom, the liberty we have in Christ, mediates between the extremes of license and legalism. It is of the essence of learning because the true learner is a humble, teachable person, free from the dictatorship of all but the truth.

### DEFINITION

Academic freedom is the freedom of the teacher to teach, of the student to learn, and of the college to be an educational institution. In a Christian college it should exemplify a Christian liberty that avoids the extremes both of legalism and of license. This suggests three possible policies: the legalistic, the libertine, and responsible freedom. Russell Kirk aptly describes them as follows:

> In the eyes of the Indoctrinators, the scholar and teacher are servants, hired for money to do a job. In the eyes of the Doctrinaire Liberals, the scholar and the teacher are masterless men, rather like Cain, and ought to remain so. In my eyes the scholar and the teacher are Bearers of the Word— that is, the conservators and promulgators of knowledge in all its forms; they are neither simply hired functionaries nor simply knights-errant in their lists.[4]

I think of the indoctrinator as the dogmatist for whom all issues are settled and all truth known and, as a result, all creative scholarship erodes away. He is the legalist who, enforcing things as they are, forgets that faith, like love, cannot be forced, but rather rises as the free response of a man to the revelation of truth, a response out of an enlightened mind freed from the shackles of opinion and prejudice. The indoctrinator has a ready-made set of answers for every question.

---

[4] *Op. cit.*, p. 31.

But when his students meet new problems or start to think for themselves, they have neither the answers nor the developed intellectual powers to work them out. Having learned neither the meaning nor the use of their freedom, they either remain shackled by fear or else become disillusioned libertines, the campus cynics whose loyalty is to themselves rather than to the God of truth. Christian indoctrination is a self-contradiction for the educator who purports to develop the individuality and intellectual powers of persons created in God's image.

On the other extreme, the "freedom bandwagon" collides head-on with the legitimate concerns of society and its institutions. The libertine interprets "education for democracy" to mean one that ensures absolute equality; no viewpoint can be more true than another: all stand on the same level and are to be presented with a benign and uncritical relativism. His presupposition is that nothing is true in itself; truth is relative, and ideas are but the tools of successful adjustment. He tries to solve problems without any fixed reference in eternal truth and unchanging values.

For those whose ultimate loyalty is to the expedient and the popular rather than to truth, Socrates would have a goading question; so would the medieval scholars, the scholarly victims of Nazi oppression, and our Christian forbears. It is the question of the apostle, "Whether it be right in the sight of God to hearken unto you more than unto God, judge ye. For we cannot but speak the things which we have seen and heard" (Acts 4:19, 20). To the libertine this must be said, for the conscience of the true scholar and the Christian teacher cannot be bound to human representations of truth, nor can the teacher so bind his students.

Liberty flourishes under neither totalitarianism nor anarchy, neither legalism nor license. It thrives under law, but is smothered in an atmosphere of fear and suspicion. Liberty is not uncommitted, but its commitment is to an ideal higher than current institutions or present laws. Academic freedom is valuable only when there is a prior commitment to the truth. And commitment to the truth is fully worthwhile only when that truth exists in One who transcends both the relativity of human perspectives and the fears of human concern.

Academic freedom may be defined, then, as freedom to explore the truth in a responsible fashion, to think, even to make mistakes and correct them; it is the freedom of the teacher to enlist his students in the same quest, and to equip them carefully for its exacting demands; it is the freedom of the student to think for himself and to disagree on reasonable grounds with what his teachers say.

The qualifying words, "responsible" and "carefully," require emphasis, for it is here that educators are most often accused of failure. The qualification implies a responsible motive, neither selfish nor narrowly partisan, but first a love for the truth and then a concern for the common good of the community to which one belongs. It implies care about attitudes, lest one grow heady and opinionated and cease to bow in humility and awe. It implies working loyally within the framework of reference to which one stands committed, rather than acting like iconoclasts or teaching subversion. The teacher in the evangelical institution operates within the framework of belief confessed by his college. In this sense the academic community is always a community of the committed.

Academic freedom is a form of "liberty under law." Law gives order and direction to liberty, protecting it against abuses from right and from left, guiding and safeguarding its proper use. The Christian educator cannot forget that his responsibility is not only to society and the church, to his students and colleagues, but also and primarily to the truth. He is constantly impressed with the fact that the Scriptures aid rather than hinder the quest for truth: they open up new and exciting perspectives for the dedicated and vigorous mind to explore.

The apostle Paul spoke of Christian liberty in relation to the "weaker brother" (I Cor. 8-9). To this weaker brother the Christian educator bears a dual responsibility. As an educator he must help him gain strength and maturity of faith and thought by offering fellowship and guidance in the exercise of liberty. Over-protection breeds weakness; repression breeds rebellion. As a Christian, however, the educator must not cause a weaker brother to stumble; he must not weaken him further, nor alienate him from the faith. In order to avoid becoming a stumbling-block the Christian educator needs to scrutinize his pedagogy, organize his curriculum, even restrict at times his own public utterances.

The customary distinction between academic and political freedom is important. What I say or do as a private citizen outside my own area of professional competence cannot be justified on the grounds of academic freedom. Nor does the American college desire the liberty intended by the German *Lehrfreiheit,* with its freedom to teach whatever I choose, whenever I choose and however I choose. That may be proper in the German university but not with the structured curriculum and stated objectives of the American liberal arts college. Nor does academic freedom give the teacher the lectern to ride his own hobbies, to proselytize for his own peculiar viewpoints, or to engage in a knock-down drag-out fight with everyone who disagrees. On some matters he may wish to keep silent, to remain noncommittal or to withhold judgment. In no case should he deliberately overstate his case or assert a degree of finality that the evidence does not justify. Responsibility and propriety require that freedom subserve the truth with complete honesty, and with loyalty to the goals of the institution a teacher serves.

There can be no skeletons in the closet, no significant alternatives ignored, no embarrassing questions barred. We need not restrict what can be taught; rather we should look at things in their historical and philosophical contexts and think in terms of world-views and cultural outlooks. We must remember that Christianity touches learning not only at obvious points of theological contact, but in the interpretation of material. We need not excise dangerous things from the curriculum; rather we should build a curriculum and a methodology by means of which anything can be properly interpreted and profitably discussed, in which students progressively make truth and value judgments of their own. They will face it all after graduation anyway, perhaps earlier. It is a tragedy when in their bull sessions and campus publications students raise questions and air ideas with a frankness they do not experience in class, and if we encourage it in class it is inconsistent to restrict it outside. Improprieties may occur to embarrass us—but students are still immature late adolescents to whom propriety comes hard. Adolescents need frank discussion and patient guidance rather than restrictions whose unexplained or inconsistent inflexibility incites reactions and builds negative temperaments. To repress student freedom of thought and expression is like brainwashing; they should rather be inspired to channel their freedom into constructive Christian thought and action.

## PROBLEMS

Two kinds of criticism are leveled at the Christian college, one from the left and one from the right. From the left comes the charge that education from a religious perspective lacks objectivity and therefore respectability. But if intellectual objectivity is presuppositionless thinking or learning without guiding purposes, then it exists neither in the Christian college nor anywhere else. Neutrality on matters of belief and value is humanly impossible. Objectivity consists rather in acknowledging and scrutinizing one's point of view and testing presuppositions. It is more a matter of honesty than of neutrality. Every scholar has his commitments. The Christian college is unique only because its faculty and administration have common commitments of a religious and moral sort, rather than the variegated commitments of a secular institution.

It is readily recognized in the literature on academic freedom that responsibility to the truth, to scholarly integrity, and to one's students goes hand in hand with academic freedom. These are commitments made tacitly or explicitly by the university teacher, yet they are held to be quite consonant with his freedom and objectivity. In the Christian college, additional theological commitments are often expected of the teacher, whether to an institutional or denominational statement of faith or in the form of his own *credo,* but these also are consonant with intellectual honesty and objectivity if the teacher is open about it and believes what he does thinkingly. Moreover, some such commitments are essential in defining the faith and making it a base from which to work at the integration of learning. The American Association of University Professors asks only that any such conditions of employment be clearly stated in writing at the time of appointment.[5]

Some church-related colleges establish no such conditions of employment, and look at them as negatively as political liberals looked at "loyalty oaths" in the McCarthy era. It is argued that, with the possible exception of its religion department, a Christian college should maintain the same religious pluralism as a public university. It would probably be wise not to have teachers openly antagonistic to the goals of the college, but otherwise even an atheist might hold a faculty position.

This viewpoint presupposes some other idea of a Christian college than that which I have been developing. It suggests intruding Christian religious instruction into the curriculum as an addendum or perhaps a catalyst for Christian thought rather than as the motivational and informative center of an entire education. It does not envision bringing the creative contribution of Christian perspectives to bear in all disciplines and all campus activities. The elaboration of a coherent worldview and the development of college life as a Christian academic community would simply not be possible under such an arrangement. This is not to say that it has no value at all, but rather that it comes closer to the idea of an institute of Christian studies on a secular campus than to an education expressive of the ultimate unity of truth in obedience to the creation mandate.

It is essential to recognize that a college is not a local church. The danger of subordinating education to indoctrination or moralizing or other activities finds an instructive parallel in the efforts of the 1960's to politicize the university. In that case the educational task was subordinated to political and social action as student groups attempted to force change. But to make the campus an arena for political action is as much a

---

[5] See the American Association of University Professors' 1940 statement reprinted in *Academic Freedom and Tenure,* ed. by Louis Joughin (Univ. of Wisconsin Press, 1967), pp. 33-39.

violation of the freedom to teach and to learn as it is to make
the campus into an indoctrination center or even a missionary
agency. Informed political and social concerns have their place
in an educational institution, and Christian conviction and witness do for Christians in any setting, but a college is still a college and academic freedom protects its right to be primarily a
place of learning.

This introduces the criticism from the right, that teachers
and students use academic freedom as a license to compromise
faith and morals, and that their freedom must therefore be
either restricted or removed. Restrictions on freedom in general develop because our world as a whole, and the church in
particular, is in trouble and life is not as free as it should
be for any of us. In the attempt to conserve the accomplish-
ments of the past, cherished social and religious institutions
and long-held particular viewpoints, there is a tendency to
deny the freedom to improve on the past, to examine and to
question.

This process is unfortunately aided by depreciating the
academic task. Who has not encountered the hardheaded businessman who smiles indulgently at the educator's idealism?
How many parents relish the fact that someone else is going
to mold Junior's mind and help determine his destiny? How
many parents fear that higher education will kill their son's
faith? How many of us, set in our ways, like our unthinking
passivity to be disturbed by some Socratic gadfly? Is it any
wonder that some people try to swat the bugs that pester them?

Academic freedom would not create such criticism if we
had ideal faculty, ideal students, ideal administrators, ideal
trustees and ideal constituencies. But this is not yet the best of
all possible worlds. The truth can surely speak for itself to
honest and mature and well-informed minds, but not all minds
are equally honest and mature and well informed, and we are
at best poor communicators.

Students are often raised on credulity, sometimes told it is
dangerous to think and to question what they are taught. Their
view of Christianity is oversimplified, their faith a response to
the stimuli of parents and pastors; it is a sword they have yet

to try and count on when they stand alone, embattled by new ideas and conflicting values. Is it any wonder that some falter, that others react against the naiveté or obscurantism they see or imagine in their backgrounds? Pedagogical care and curriculum revision alone cannot keep them from this, nor can restrictions on their freedom to read widely and to think for themselves, for now they are growing up and being invited to join the human race in their own right. Yet college is a place to think, to raise questions and doubts and discuss them openly, and the Christian college must encourage students to do so in dialog with more mature minds, and to confront the best information and arguments available.

Trustees may come from similar backgrounds, successful professionals and businessmen, properly respected for what they have accomplished in their own fields of endeavor. They may be well equipped to handle financial investments, well able to project institutional expansion, but in educational matters many of them remain novices. In some cases they hold no more than a baccalaureate degree; some less. Yet they are called upon to make strategic decisions affecting the educational work of the college. Their understanding of educational philosophy, the value they place on academic freedom, and their theological insight and balance are frequently impoverished. Unless a trustee chooses to withhold judgment, or takes the time and effort to think through educational philosophy and related issues, he will by default be prone to blunder, and not least in actions affecting academic freedom, its existence and its implementation. Public relations considerations sometimes conflict with educational considerations. An ill-informed decision is often worse than no decision at all.

This is a peculiar plight of the American college. German universities are state institutions, theoretically free from political domination, despite their spotty history. The British university is operated by the faculty themselves, who control every aspect of college life and work. Whether or not this is desirable, the facts of life for us are different, and these facts reinforce the sacred responsibility of all those concerned.

What can be done about it? It is time that evangelical educators took the initiative in educating the evangelical public as to the nature of Christian higher education and the role of academic freedom. A college is not a church. The educator's speeches and sermons and articles as well as the college's advertisements and catalogs and brochures could expound more eloquently than they do the idea of a Christian college and the responsible use to which it tries to put its freedom.

Administrators and trustees, moreover, must protect responsible freedom against attacks from right and left. They must stand by the professor under criticism and treat him with the highest personal and ethical consideration. They must ensure him at all times the respect and dignity that befits a man of integrity, a loyal citizen, a devout believer, a gentleman and a scholar. They must support the right of students to learn, to express their ideas, and to take reasoned exception to what they are told.

To this end it must be clearly recognized that intellectual gestation (to use Socrates' figure of midwifery), while unavoidably necessary and delightfully rewarding, can still be a dangerous and painful process. The incidence of miscarriages is to be reduced, not by further restriction on the attendant doctor, but by encouraging him to face facts honestly, to look into problems with the penetration of x-rays, to develop responsible techniques based on well-informed understanding and thoroughly critical research. Education, like having babies, is a calculated risk. Education is not like training: most children can be successfully trained, but not all babies are successfully delivered. Yet both education and having babies are part of the divine mandate to replenish and subdue the earth and have dominion in God's creation.

# 7 THE COLLEGE COMMUNITY

Traditionally, the American college operated *in loco parentis,* exercising authority over the personal lives as well as the academic pursuits of students in behalf of their parents. This concept became impracticable in the increasingly large universities of the mid-twentieth century, and increased emphasis on student rights along with precedent-setting court cases have brought it into question. Totally removed from *in loco parentis,* the "university without walls" makes degree-earning studies possible for people who are unable to become resident students or even to attend courses.

*In loco parentis* meant that American colleges accepted responsibility for all sides of student life. The Christian college has not abandoned that notion, but nowadays it is more often expressed in the idea of a college community. Involvement in the life of a community is a large part of what attracts students to small colleges, for faculty-student relations are often closer and opportunities for campus leadership, athletic participation and such like are more readily available than in large universities. The Christian college, moreover, is largely a community of Christians whose intellectual and social and cultural life is influenced by Christian values, so that the learning situation is life as a whole approached from a Christian point of view. It is a situation calculated to teach young people to relate everything to their faith.

## THE IDEA OF COMMUNITY

A Christian community need not be an unrealistic environment, for as long as human beings, Christians included, are immature, fallible and prone to sin, and as long as the college community maintains lively interaction with the non-Christian world, the campus remains far from any otherworldly utopia. To my mind, the main dangers facing a Christian college community are rather those confronting any community: excessive individualism and excessive administrative control.

Excessive individualists tend to behave like Robinson Crusoes, each on his own island trying to find himself by doing his own insular thing, as if it were possible for him in either life or thought to cut himself off from society. Man is intrinsically a social being. The life of a hermit is less than human. Yet some tend to shun community by losing themselves in the anonymity of a large university, and some by non-involvement in the religious, political or social life of the campus. Some do so by closing their minds to other people's ideas. The person who treats the liberal arts as largely irrelevant chooses the life of an intellectual hermit. The person who regards the past as unrelated to his own life is a historical hermit, living in isolation from others. The person who values doing his own thing without regard for more universal and lasting values is an ethical hermit.

The opposite danger is that a college impose its ways on unwilling members, frustrating them as individuals and stunting their growth by forcing them into institutional patterns. Excessive controls occur in the political realm in totalitarian societies; they occur in the home in the case of unreasonably dictatorial parents who cannot let Johnny grow up and be himself; they would occur in a school if it prescribed dress codes, dormitory hours and other behavioral standards in such a casuistical fashion as to leave no room for different life-styles or for individual choice. Both extremes exhibit a misunderstanding of the nature of human community and the social nature of individuals.

Seventeenth- and eighteenth-century philosophers sometimes talk as if man is by nature an individualist who could lead a fully human life without social institutions, a Robinson Crusoe without intrinsic need for Friday or anyone else. The family and the state are not part of the created order, but rather a later product of individual self-interest accommodating itself to other people. On the other hand, Greek and Roman philosophers recognized that man is by nature a social being, and that this is inseparable from his rational nature. According to the Old Testament, God knew from the beginning that it was not good for a man to be alone. Nobody can live with meaning entirely for himself. We are what we are and become what we become through the influence of parents, friends, schooling, church and so on. Probably the peer group is the greatest single influence in shaping young people of high school and college age. But in any case we are social beings in our very nature, created to live in communion with God and community with men.

Whatever a man is, he is through his relationships with others. He develops intellectually as he learns from others (and the dormitory "bull session" is often as important to his growth as the classroom). His history is that of his society; his values are shaped by others and shape others in turn; he exercises his freedom with regard for the freedom of others. Because a man's rational and historical and valuational nature all require societal life, it follows that to develop those aspects of a man a liberal education can best be conducted within a community.

Community arises from the social nature of men whose common stake in life and common values unite them in a common task. When a community organizes its life to preserve or enhance or transmit those values or to undertake its task more effectively, institutions arise. They are ordered communities with an outward structure of rules and procedures intended to implement an inner community of interest and purpose. We have institutions of various sorts: domestic, political, economic and religious as well as educational. In any institution rules or laws are established to implement its goals while preserving the rights and furthering the interests of its members individually and collectively.

Individualism therefore becomes excessive when individuals without essential community of value and purpose fragment the life and frustrate the goals of an institution. Each must realize that he cannot achieve his ends in isolation from, or at cross-purposes with, the institutions of which he is part. Administrative controls become excessive when they no longer express any underlying community of interest and purpose nor allow for individual differences that are compatible with the common purpose.

## THE BASIS OF COMMUNITY

Campus talk often claims that love creates community, that unless people feel warmly toward each other all the time, there is no community. This is mistaken on two counts. First, it confuses love with feeling. Christian love is a moral virtue, not just, and sometimes not at all, a warm quality to one's feelings. It is the sort of moral concern for others' well-being that motivates hard and sacrificial work. What love does on the inward side of human relations, justice attempts on the outward side by securing people's rights and opportunities as equitably as possible. Love, then, is not community-feeling but an inner moral attitude and commitment.

Second, to say that love creates community, when "love" denotes liking and feeling, puts the cart before the horse. It is not feelings of love that create community, but community that creates feelings of love. Our likes and dislikes grow out of our experiences and for that reason feelings are fickle: they fluctuate up and down with health and digestion and climate and a myriad other incidentals. But in working together at their marriage, a couple's feelings are nourished and grow; in working together in the life of a church, feelings of warmth and togetherness are enhanced; an athletic team will often talk of a feeling of oneness that grows out of shared experiences. And the feeling of community on campus is enriched when students, faculty and administration are all heartily involved in their common educational task.

What does create a community if it is not common feeling? Community is created by values and purposes and a common task. Paul described the unity of the church with all its rich diversity of gifted individuals in terms of the faith and the mandate that gave the church reason to exist. What holds a marriage together are the values and goals a couple share, not primarily either their feelings or their marriage contract. The things that

unite a nation are its common heritage and ideals. For man
is a rational and valuing being whose understanding and purposes guide the ways in which he participates with others in
shaping his own history. This is what makes men individuals
in community.

The college is a community, an academic community. Its
unifying task is education. How a student may feel about a
teacher or administrator or about rules and requirements is
secondary to his moral commitment to that task. I do not expect students to like everything about me or my courses or
the college, but I do expect them to be committed to gaining
an education. It is that which qualifies them as members of an
academic community.

We do well to remind ourselves that as an academic community a Christian college is not a local church—although it
it important that its students and teachers worship together.
Nor is it an athletic or social club—although physical and
social development have an important place. Nor is it a service agency—although people serve others in need both on and
off campus. Nor is it a vocational training school—although
liberal learning is excellent preparation for many a job and
vocational preparation may well grow out of the liberal arts.
The educational task is what creates the Christian college community; it, not chapel services or social service or athletics or
dates or job training, is its overall purpose and reason for
existence. The Christian college is of course a community of
faith as well as learning, but the two are not disconnected;
rather they are to be integrated so that faith gives direction
and meaning to learning. The goal is still educational, and
membership in a Christian college community presupposes
commitment to that end.

This basis for community has implications for student recruitment and admissions. It makes it inconsistent to recruit
students primarily for athletic purposes or by advertising opportunities for extracurricular Christian service or other activities. If we are inviting people to join a Christian academic
community we should say so, and say why it is important,
rather than putting second things first. While not all bait de-

ceives, baiting the hook deceptively may be acceptable in catching fish, but it is unethical in selling things to people and in recruiting students.

College admission should mean that a person qualifies for membership in an academic community. Academic records, including abilities and aptitudes and interests, should be emphasized in order to determine a candidate's potential, rather than simply his past performance. But liberal education is concerned with the whole person and his possible contributions in service to God and men: the selection process should therefore look for creative ability rather than simply a record of following routine instructions and assimilating standard information. We must resist the temptation to enroll students for the sake of filling enrollment quotas and balancing budgets. Budgets and quotas should be set with the realization that not everyone who applies should necessarily go to college.

Does a Christian academic community have to be a community of Christians? Should only Christian students be admitted? No Christian college to my knowledge has the same theological requirements for prospective students as it does for its faculty, and rightly so. A teacher should be mature enough to have considered the major areas of Christian theology for himself, but hardly so for a student. A teacher needs to understand the faith he seeks to relate to his discipline, but a student comes to learn both about the faith and about the various disciplines and about their relationship.

Some Christian colleges, however, prefer to admit only students who give evidence of personal Christian commitment. Undoubtedly this offers a common basis for exploring the faith and its relations to life and learning, so that primary attention can be given to constructive educational endeavors without the distraction of apologetic and other debates erupting at every juncture. The campus community then has an explicit core of belief and values, however little understood, to which appeal can be made in encouraging learning and shaping campus life. In such cases the practice of Christian community can find creative expression and have a profound impact on the whole life of its members.

Other Christian colleges, for a variety of reasons, have a religiously mixed student body. In some cases a denominational school has to accept all applicants from its supporting denomination, and a church upbringing is of course no guarantee of Christian commitment and values. In some, economic reasons cause a college to recruit students, frequently from the local community, regardless of their religious outlook. In some there is the measured policy of selecting a percentage of uncommitted applicants, partly for evangelistic purposes and partly for the educational value of a realistic exposure to non-Christian as well as Christian points of views.

In such cases, the idea of a Christian academic community needs to be conceived, not as a community of common faith, but rather in terms of a core-community of faith that in love embraces others in the dialog of its life and thought. The campus climate and student life-styles will inevitably reflect the difference. Even so, the college should be frank with all its students that life and thought will deliberately be explored from a Christian perspective, and that the Christian faith itself will become a focal point in their education. The admissions process should at least ensure an acceptance of these facts.

## A CLIMATE OF FAITH AND LEARNING

How the idea of college community is implemented varies somewhat from college to college. Unity of purpose does not imply unanimity either within one college or within the community of Christian colleges. There must always be room for individuality and heterogeneity, for lively disagreement and dialog are essential to personal growth and institutional vitality.

When it comes to implementation, the college community must work at what Ordway Tead called a "climate of learning." In the Christian college this should be extended to a "climate of faith and learning." Centuries ago Plato inquired whether virtue can be taught, and decided that if virtue is a form of knowledge it can be taught like anything else. But a positive Christian attitude to liberal learning, while a virtue, is not a form of knowledge to be taught that simply. The instructional process cannot ensure it. Yet the climate of a community helps create attitudes and impart values. A community that reflects and speaks and prays about what it is trying to do, that structures its life accordingly and enjoys itself in the process, creates levels of expectation.

We need to ask how values are transmitted. Young people assimilate them more from example than precept, more from their peers than from their elders, and more by being involved than by being spectators. Values can be caught from the contagious example of a community at work, in this case a community of enthusiastic and well-equipped scholars who infect their students with a love for learning and involve them in disciplined work. As teachers inspire students and students infect other students, a climate of learning emerges.

The teacher is the key to a climate of learning. His teaching is his ministry. His enthusiasm about ideas, his scholarship, and the importance he places on teaching provide a model. The Christian college has escaped the "publish or perish" syndrome, but this never justifies the opposite extreme of abandoning creative intellectual work. The teacher must keep up in his field and be involved in professional organizations; to grow he needs to expand his knowledge by research. Given the ability, the Christian professor has the same moral responsibility as other scholars to publish in his field, along with the added responsibility of developing Christian perspectives when they are pertinent to what he writes. His example helps create a climate of faith and learning in the college community.

Teaching is an exacting art that requires physical health, emotional balance and mental acumen. The teacher of all people must therefore steward his personal resources for the job. His most disagreeable task—grading papers—is often one of the most important things he does. Grading has two purposes, evaluation and criticism. Evaluation is for the record that graduate schools and employers examine. Criticism is for the student's education. A paper that takes a student's time and best abilities deserves careful analysis. Detailed annotations and constructive suggestions will push him further than he previously thought possible and can sometimes teach him more than he learned from writing the paper in the first place.

It is important that the teacher be transparently Christian as well as an enthusiastic and careful scholar, and that he not compartmentalize the two but think integrationally himself. How he contributes to the campus climate may vary, for pedagogy is in large measure relative to personality, and lecturing can excite and involve the student as effectively as discussions and coffee hours, as long as it is not a substitute for careful student interaction with source materials. It is the person of the teacher rather than a particular gimmick or method that counts. As in Phillips Brooks' classic definition of preaching, so too teaching conveys "truth through personality."

A community that argues ideas only in the classroom, a teacher whose work seems a chore, a student who never reads a thing beyond what is assigned, a campus that empties itself of life and thought all weekend, an attitude that devaluates disciplined study in comparison with rival claimants on time and energy, a dominant concern for job-preparation—these can never produce a climate of learning.

In his *Republic,* Plato urged selectivity in the use of literature and the arts because they too transmit values. We need not agree with Plato's censorship to realize that when a good writer involves his readers or a good artist captures his audience he makes them feel as well as know the values he expresses. Exciting art and literature are like a captivating teacher in the effect they have on students; they too can generate a love of learning.

So can the college chapel service that is a regular part of community life in the Christian college. It should not be peripheral to the educational task but should constantly renew the vision of a Christian mind. When the well-intentioned speaker discourages intellectual pursuits or cultural involvements or political action, he turns off many students. Chapel speakers should realize that a Christian college exists to cultivate the intellect and involve people in their culture, and that it is therefore more than a conserving influence in the world. A college is Christian in that it does its work in a Christian way, not by encouraging an unthinking faith to counterbalance faithless thought. If education is God's present calling to students, then no question arises about whether God or studies come first, for God is to be honored in and through studies. Compartmentalization has no place on the Christian campus.

A college chapel service that renews this vision and keeps things in focus is essential in cultivating a climate of faith and learning. It is the college community at worship, cultivating Christian devotion, dedicating all its activities to the glory of God, seeking biblical instruction that will guide its life and thought, and reflecting on its God-given calling.

## COLLEGE LIFE-STYLE

Life itself is more than learning and worship, and so is life in college. The Christian college has its religious, social, artistic, athletic, political and journalistic activities—all the things people normally do together. Each makes its own contribution and each affords opportunities to grow in reflective understanding and in community with other people. But the extracurricular can easily become remote from the spirit of inquiry that prevails in the classroom. Political groups can campaign and dogmatize without really examining the positions they endorse, and the campus newspaper can give scant evidence of its academic environment. A Christian liberal arts education must extend its threefold humanizing emphasis into the extracurricular: a rational examination of ideas must prevail over uncritical dogmatism, a sense of history must replace the shortsightedness of "relevance," and the same reasoned value judgments should be expected as are cultivated in the classroom. And in all activities it should be remembered that the college's concern for the whole person extends to the development of Christian faith, devotion, dedication and character. Classes and extracurricular activities can contribute, as well as chapel and other religious events.

Perhaps the most debated ingredient is a college's rules of conduct. Nobody likes to be told what he may or may not do, especially the college student achieving adulthood. Several observations should be kept in mind. First, every institution has rules and regulations, and necessarily so for the orderly and effective pursuit of its goals as well as for the safeguarding of

individual rights. The difference between arbitrary and meaningful rules lies in the relationship they have to the values,
purposes and work of the community. What do the rules contribute? Some tend to persist that are products of the past or
of inept conceptions of college. What is debatable is accordingly not whether a college should have rules, but rather what
particular rules are appropriate.

Second, rules should be formulated and administered with
the realization that the lives of late adolescents and young
adults in today's world can no longer be regulated, if ever
they could, so as to protect them from immoral practices and
otherwise harmful things. Rather, young people must be taught
to exercise their individual liberties wisely, with moral principle, restraint and Christian concern. Campus rules should
provide both an example of and an encouragement to this.

Third, the rules governing a Christian college community,
like those governing other institutions, are of three sorts: some
reflect existing civil legislation, some are ethical (regarding
extramarital sex, cheating, drunkenness, etc.), some are prudential and operational (parietal hours, no alcoholic beverages,
etc.). Discussion focuses on the last two, yet not so much on
whether life itself is subject to moral and prudential judgments
as on whether an institution should legislate such matters. Here
the Christian college parts company with many a university, for
its Christian identity implies the same concern for Christian
morality and prudence as was evident in early Christian communities in the New Testament, There, persistent and flagrant
breaches of God's moral law called for church discipline, and
prudence was strongly urged on the church in other than moral
matters. This affords biblical basis for institutional rules regarding moral conduct, although it is not as clear whether explicit rules or just adult counsel should apply in matters of
prudence.

Fourth, every community has mores embodying past judgments, tacit or explicit, on prudential matters affecting the purposes for which it exists. While mores change with time and
vary from subgroup to subgroup, it is still true that to participate in community life one has in general to adopt its mores.

The same pattern applies in the Christian community, including its evangelical subgroup, although noticeable variations distinguish Reformed from pietist segments. The Christian college belongs to the Christian community as well as the academic world. The mores of the evangelical community are therefore evident in college mores, and so in college rules.

Far more important than the specific rules enforced is their relation to the task of forming Christian men and women concerned about weightier matters of the law and about the dominant moral and social ills of the day, who exercise their freedom in good judgment and wise action. It should be observed that the mores of the church often arose out of concern over such things as sexual looseness and drunkenness, and served to create an alternative life-style that was more authentically Christian. Both the Reformed and the Anabaptist traditions share this concern although they express it in different ways: the one in terms of the cultural mandate and the other in terms of the witness of an ethic of love as an alternative to prevalent social morality. In these terms the life of a Christian college community poses an alternative to the lifestyle in much of academia today. Its prudential rules, though not perfect, express a Christian concern that goes the second mile in purposeful self-restraint. In the final analysis the purpose should be not so much protective as educative, to cultivate Christian graces and create alternatives to the way people live in a non-Christian world.

# 8 THE USES OF A CHRISTIAN COLLEGE

To this point we have concentrated on the intrinsic values of Christian liberal arts education, but the liberal arts are also useful. In this concluding chapter we shall consider their instrumental worth. Granted that the basic question to ask about an education is what it can do to me, many people persist in asking how they can use it. This is especially true during job shortages in the professions, or when life's horizons do not extend beyond earning a living. It is increasingly true in the 1970's: how can young people whose approach to life is experiential rather than rational be expected to value intellectual discipline? If their outlook is ahistorical, how can they be expected to want historical perspective? And since they tend to be relativistic, how can they appreciate the traditional values of the cultural heritage? Are contemporary young people sufficiently rational and historical and valuational beings to have much use for liberal education?

The difficulty is qualitatively similar to what teachers have faced for years. In general Americans approach life pragmatically, and their young people have come to college for pragmatic purposes for at least as long as I have been teaching. It is nothing new for a philosophy teacher to be asked how philosophy majors ever use what they learn, or for the self-made businessman to demand of his son how he expects all that literature and art and history to earn him a living.

Such people have a limited concept of life's vocation, and are not readily convinced that jobs and skills are secondary to the larger end of stretching one's capacities and becoming more fully human. If their own lives still focus on lesser ends, they cannot readily grasp our abstractions. But the fact is that a liberal education has many uses, precisely because its main contribution is to persons.

## EDUCATION FOR WORK

First of all, and despite the fact that the Christian vocation for which a Christian college prepares young people is vastly more than earning a living, it does equip them for a life's work. Liberal arts education is a non-professional and non-vocational preparation for any profession or vocation that demands critical judgment, a sense of history, decision-making ability, an understanding of society and of other people—in fact the very qualities that liberal education is intended to cultivate. The medical man needs to understand not only chemistry and biology and psychology, but himself and other people and the world that helps make them what they are; otherwise he becomes an insensitive mechanic of the human body. And increasingly he must prepare himself in such areas of medical ethics as abortion, euthanasia, and genetic control: civil legislation is after all no guide to Christian ethics. The elementary teacher needs, as a basis for her teaching methods and child psychology, an understanding of the nature of persons and their education, of family and community structures, an appreciation of what makes good art and literature good, the ability to nourish creativity and critical thinking through her own creative and critical powers. The businessman needs more than fast talk or organizational ability: he needs a view of work that will make his efforts more human and more moral, an understanding of the economy, and the ability to develop leadership potential in his associates. And the minister and missionary need a great deal more than a good grasp of Scripture, the habit of prayer, and a way with words and people: they need an understanding of human beings that is enriched by the humanities, historical perspective on the church and its theology, and insight into the social and intellectual issues with which people are grappling today. It is not by accident that medical schools, law schools and theological seminaries are for college graduates, and that business enterprises frequently employ the liberal arts major who can think for himself and who can later secure an M.B.A. degree.

When we think of the Christian's obligation to practice the Lordship of Christ in all he does, we realize the need for Christian physicians to whom healing is a God-given ministry to be performed with wisdom and love, for Christian teachers who see for themselves and help others to see the difference that Christianity makes to life and learning, and for Christian businessmen struggling to apply Christian ethics in their legal transactions and personnel policies. What we need, then, is an education that prepares one to be thoughtfully and consistently Christian in his work, in other words a Christian liberal arts education.

A liberal education offers a world-view and a sharpened mind for all sorts of work, but two more specific contributions must be noted: one is the historical and theoretical foundations of a particular profession, and the other is ethical. The first can be seen in the case of teacher preparation. The present trend is toward behaviorally described, performance-oriented goals, and the curricular direction is away from theoretical and historical foundations. This should not surprise us at a time when the behavioral sciences have achieved a large popular following. Yet it is essential to realize that however important performance standards may be, and however much such skills need sharpening, the human person to be educated is far more than the theoretical behaviorist allows and than behavioral science can measure. Phenomenologists, both in philosophy and in the behavioral sciences, point to the larger experience of our humanness within which behavioral accounts need to be located, and from any Christian perspective a behaviorist's view of man is grossly inadequate and oversimplified. It follows that teacher preparation should involve more than behavioral objectives. Teaching methods and other immediately useful things should grow from an understanding of the psychology and sociology of learning that has been carefully scrutinized in the light of historical, philosophical and theological perspectives. In a Christian liberal arts college these foundations must be explicit and the would-be teacher must be forced to grapple with them. It is here, in issues about the nature of man and his knowledge and his self-discovery, that the Christian faith makes contact with the work of education, and that faith and learning are open to integration. In other words, the philosophy of education can be examined in larger philosophical context, and the history of education in larger historical context, and the psychology of learning in larger psychological context, and all of it in a theological context, when it is studied in a Christian liberal arts college.

Another example is the legal profession. American law schools tend to approach legal education on a pragmatic and conventional basis. That is to say, the law represents a consensus of popular opinion, rooted in a more general consensus and ultimately in the Constitution. It develops and changes with public opinion. No Christian should rest content with such a view of law. Indeed, both Christianity and other historical influences in our political heritage rest law ultimately not on the Constitution but on universal human rights given by God to man. Without some such basis for law, the legislative process can become a pragmatic juggling of power over public opinion in the attempt to secure partisan ends for one group or another. To prepare for the legal profession, then, the student must be exposed to its historical and theoretical foundations in political and legal philosophy, and ultimately in a biblical view of man and government. This is what makes a Christian liberal arts college useful to the would-be Christian lawyer.

The second evident use of a liberal education is in the area of ethics. In the last few years we have been confronted by one agonizing moral issue after another: Vietnam and Cambodia, then Watergate and the whole area of political morality in relation to the law, not to mention abortion and other matters of medical ethics. The parade will continue. Yet every citizen faces these issues and, we are told, the jury is the American people. In the conduct of our work, as well as of our citizenship, we are forced to make moral judgments. Businessmen and lawyers and doctors, teachers and strikers and ecologists— we make judgments for ourselves and for others. Yet ill-informed judgments spell disaster. Ethical education—of the sort a Christian college can and should offer—is essential to the moral conduct of work.

## EDUCATION FOR LEISURE

The workweek is shortening, in some cases to four days, and early retirement is a frequent option. Modern man has more opportunity for leisure than his predecessors, but unless he can use it for personal growth and the enrichment of others he is likely to laze away his years in self-indulgence or on trivia. In the past we have been so busy working and so controlled by some sort of work-ethic, biblical or not, that scant attention has been given either to preparing for leisure or to a play-ethic.

Obviously, enjoyment is not wrong and all of us need rest and recreation. But in an increasingly leisured society, unless a man's world is larger than his work and more varied than TV and fishing, life will grow increasingly thin and empty. The hedonist, who makes pleasure the highest end of man, faces the paradox that the more he seeks pleasure the more it eludes him. When pleasure becomes the highest end of leisure time, it confronts the same paradox: the more time I have for pleasure and the more effort I give to seeking it, the more evasive it becomes.

> I said to myself, "Come now, I will make a test of pleasure; enjoy yourself." But behold, this also was vanity. . . . I made great works; I built houses and planted vineyards for myself; I made myself gardens and parks, and planted in them all kinds of fruit trees. I made myself pools from which to water the forest of growing trees. I bought male and female slaves, and had slaves who were born in my house; I had also great possessions of herds and flocks, more than any who had been before me in Jerusalem. I also gathered for myself silver and gold and the treasure of kings and provinces; I got singers, both men and women, and many concubines, man's delight. . . . And whatever my eyes desired I did not keep from them; I kept my heart from no pleasure, for my heart found pleasure in all my toil, and this was my reward for all my toil. Then I considered all that my hands had done and the toil I had spent in doing

it, and behold, all was vanity and a striving after wind, and there was nothing to be gained under the sun (Eccl. 2:1, 4-8, 10-11 RSV).

To avoid this hedonic paradox in a leisured society, we need a large enough view of life and its purpose to generate meaningful and enriching activities. Not only our work should glorify God, but also our leisure; not only our work can be a service to others, but also our leisure; not only our work should stretch us and help build character, but also our leisure.

Consequently we need more than job training. We need an education that lays a foundation for the wise and creative use of leisure and for a lifetime of enriching reading and learning, an education that helps us to understand and appreciate a wide variety of the worthwhile things life holds and that enables us to bring Christian perspectives to bear on our participation in social and cultural and other activities.

### EDUCATION FOR CITIZENSHIP

President Kennedy, in a speech in 1961 at the University of North Carolina, pointed out that our nation's first great leaders were liberally educated men, and claimed that "this versatility, this vitality, this intellectual energy, put to the service of our country, represents our greatest resource." He added, ". . . how much we still need the men and women educated in the liberal tradition, willing to take the long look, undisturbed by the prejudices and slogans of the moment, who attempt to make an honest judgment on difficult events."[1]

Participatory democracy requires an educated citizenship. Voting and grass-roots political involvement, not to mention participation in local government, school boards and a host of other things, demand not just information but the ability to interpret information, to research an issue, to criticize a position, to make value judgments, to anticipate the future on the basis of the past, to formulate reasonable objectives and to lay plans accordingly.

---

[1] Quoted in *Time,* Oct. 20, 1961.

The role of the Christian citizen is especially sensitive. He cannot expect to legislate distinctively Christian positions on the moral issues of the day, but he must endeavor to influence legislation, policy formation and public administration from the local up to the national level. We need Christian legislators and public servants who will bring high demands for integrity and openness to politics, but they must also be men of ability. Christian colleges should be producing a steady flow of highly motivated people entering public service at every level of government.

## EDUCATION FOR CHURCHMANSHIP

We have heard in recent years of the church's failure to speak with a prophetic voice about the moral issues of the day. We are told that the Christian message has not been addressed to the mind of modern man. To whatever extent the criticisms hold—and this is no place to assess them—they underscore the need for clergy and laymen who understand the world in which they live, who are concerned about matters of social morality, and who can think and speak what they believe in cogent and creative ways.

The local church will fail to communicate to thinking men and women if it either does not know or does not care what they are thinking, nor understand how the Christian message touches their concerns. The preacher can criticize views that nobody any longer holds and fail to make contact with issues that really grip the contemporary mind, unless he himself is liberally educated and still reading and growing. The Christian layman, whose daily contact with non-Christians should illuminate what he does in the church, will find himself bewildered by conflicts of ideas and changing values unless he has the education he needs. The Christian college has the opportunity to develop in future churchmen some of these intellectual and cultural tools. It can cultivate a healthy respect for and honest understanding of the non-Christian mind through the humanities and the sciences, and on that basis expose more clearly and completely the relevance of the Christian message. Not surprisingly many evangelical leaders in foreign missions and at home, in Christian journalism and in scholarship, received their college education and their vision in Christian colleges.

The relevance of Christian higher education to life should inspire vision. I dream about Christian college students and their future roles in life. I dream of those who go on to graduate school to teach at the college level, and I see them as a generation of Christian scholars and teachers strategically located in the colleges and universities of this and other lands, penetrating the thought-patterns of their culture with Christian beliefs and values. I dream of those who go into law and medicine, into business and education, into the armed forces, into government, into marriage, and I envision their influence in reviving the Christian foundations of Western society. I dream of those who go on to seminary to preach and teach the Word of God and I pray that they may bring to the church a new sense of relevance. I look for the voice of the prophet, speaking from the evangelical pulpit about the sins of society: economic injustice, violence and sexual license, self-indulgent affluence, power struggles in politics, education and business. I look for the prophet calling men to turn repentingly to God and to practice justice and compassion not only in this land but among the nations. I dream of the massive impact for truth and righteousness that God can make both in this world and for eternity through them, with their educational opportunities.

## EDUCATION AND THE ALIENATION OF MAN

In addition to particular areas in which liberal education is of use, we face a far more basic crisis in Western culture. Two of its major symptoms are the alienation of man and the fragmentation of life. I am not concerned now with the particular alienations we experience, between husband and wife or parent and child or labor and capital or blacks and whites, nor with the processes of conflict-resolution that are needed. That is a sociological subject. I am concerned rather with man's alienation from his essential humanity, the existential alienation of which particular alienations may in large measure be symptoms.

The existentialists did not create the problem. They only dramatized it. Sociologists, too, have offered a description. Mass society with its overpopulated cities tends so to depersonalize life that we struggle to retain individual identity and dignity. We are caught up in the crowd and swept into anonymity. A technological society with highly organized administrative machinery tends to computerize everything we put into life or get out of it, and to think more of production quotas than of human values. A secularized society without religious faith has lost the hope that guarantees fulfilments still unseen. When God is dead, then the image of God in man dies too.

The result is a day in which many find their work boring and pointless, in which overproduction gluts our stores and pollutes our countryside, so that material things lose their glamor. For the materially minded, what then is man? About one marriage in two ends in divorce, while others take sexual experimentation for granted and seek the meaning of sex through improved pleasure-giving techniques. What does this say of the nature of man? Violence erupts on our streets even when we quell it on the battlefield. For the peaceably minded, what hope has man? Civil order is flaunted by the radical, but law and political morality are violated by the establishment. Life seems a mess, a tragic joke pulled by some malign demon playing cat and mouse with mankind. Sartre depicts man shipwrecked, adrift in a boat without rudder or compass, on an ocean that has no bounds. This is human life.

The alienation of man from his true existence, aggravated beyond reason in overpopulated, technological, secular society, is perhaps the most powerful single challenge facing the Christian college in today's world. The challenge is not simply to restate with firmness a Christian view of man and the message that God's grace restores men to themselves. That message is true, but its relevance has to be explicated in detail. The challenge is first to understand man's existential alienation, its complex causes and its effect on other and more particular alienations, to enter empathetically into the human predicament until we grasp its agonizing extent and ineradicable complexity, and then to understand how the Christian message addresses alienated man in his concrete situation. The student must understand the doctrines of creation and incarnation, sin and redemption, thoroughly and at their biblical source; he must wrestle with what theologians saw of their relevance in past history if he is to fully appreciate their bearing on our day.

Liberal education is a catalyst: existential questions are explored in the arts and arise when the sciences are seen in relationship to men. Liberal learning exposes to scrutiny past replies to existential questions, and some of the resources we need for grappling with them anew. But if the Christian believes that only a Christian response is ultimately sufficient, then the Christian college must help people understand in detail and in depth why and how this is so; it must inject the Christian response into contemporary thought and culture through the creative and scholarly efforts of its faculty and the influence of its graduates.

## EDUCATION AND FRAGMENTED LIVING

C. P. Snow complained some years ago in *The Two Cultures* of a communications gap at Oxford between science and the humanities. That gap is but an index to more far-ranging fragmentation. As academic disciplines have proliferated over the last century, they have compartmentalized themselves. Philosophy is one of the worst offenders: once the purveyor and critic of world-views to generations of college students, it has so given itself to technical analyses of obscure points and to commenting on others' commentaries on still others' expositions that it has earned the disrespect of undergraduates for its obscurity and irrelevance. By its default, learning is now too often meted out in compartmentalized fragments rather than as a meaningful whole.

Mass production has fragmented work. Instead of the skilled craftsman taking pride in his finished product, human automata crank handles on production lines with little sense for the whole. This is a day of specialization, not only in production but in sales, in maintenance, in medicine and law, and perhaps unavoidably so. But it hardly enhances the unity of life.

Urbanization has accelerated the process. The inner city has become a world by itself, qualitatively as well as geographically separated from the suburbs, and again from the farm. For city workers who commute, religion belongs where they live, with the women and children, so that in Gibson Winter's terminology the churches are caught in a "suburban captivity" and, with rare exceptions, hardly touch urban and business life at all.

The bits and pieces of a man's life pull him in a hundred directions, unless he has within himself something to hold them together. But our day has no integrating world-view. There was a time when the religious outlook unified life in Western society. Think of the British or European countryside: the first sign of an approaching town is the church spire that soars above everything else and around which, it seems, the whole community once clustered. In place of this we now have the high-rise, the factory belt or the corn silo, symbols of our materialism, or the sprawling metropolis that has no unifying theme unless it be the decentralized existence of fragmented man. It is as if we had been given a jigsaw puzzle to do, a thousand pieces that may not even be intended to fit together and make sense at all. Yet we live with the puzzle by day and it haunts us by night, and what meaning life has depends on the hope that it be completed.

Liberal education is concerned to see life whole. Art and literature and philosophy express world-views that can still be etched in today. One difficulty is that modern man thinks all world-views are relative, products of history that cannot transcend the past or make sense out of today and tomorrow. The evolutionary model has injured our ability to think that truth lasts forever. Yet the Christian college affirms that God transcends history while acting in it, and has spoken truth that lasts. While the Christian college therefore helps the student to understand the alternatives contemporary man faces and to appreciate why these commend themselves as powerfully as they do, it must also give itself to showing wherein Christianity is to be preferred. This means elaborating in detail a Christian world and life view that will unite the heritage of the past with the realities of the present, and draw life's fragments into the meaningful whole God intended it to be.

Finally, it might seem appropriate to speak of the future of the Christian college. I prefer otherwise, partly because prediction is so difficult but more because my hopes are not so much for the college as for its contribution to the lives of people and the history of our times. The Christian college embodies a strategy for Christian involvement in the life of the mind and the life of a culture, a believing response to the creation mandate God has given men. I have spoken of its uses and of the strategic possibilities it holds. What remains is that we grasp these possibilities, refine the idea still further, and devote our energies to implementing it more effectively tomorrow. It is a small drop in the bucket of higher education, but a drop can cause a ripple, a ripple can grow into a wave, and a wave into a flood that changes the tide of events. If the Christian college can help create a ripple of truth, it can then leave the waves and the tides to God.

# SUGGESTIONS FOR FURTHER READING

Aiken, H. D. *Predicament of the University*. Bloomington: Indiana Univ. Press, 1971.

Averill, Lloyd J. *A Strategy for the Protestant College*. Philadelphia: Westminster, 1966.

Baly, Dennis. *Academic Illusion*. Greenwich, Conn.: Seabury, 1961.

Calvin College Curriculum Study Committee. *Christian Liberal Arts Education*. Grand Rapids, Mich.: Calvin College and Wm. B. Eerdmans Publ. Co., 1970.

Ditmanson, H. H.; Hong, H. V.; and Quanbeck, W. A. *Christian Faith and the Liberal Arts*. Minneapolis, Minn.: Augsburg, 1960.

Ferré, Nels F. S. *Christian Faith and Higher Education*. New York: Harper, 1954.

Gaebelein, Frank. *The Pattern of God's Truth*. Chicago: Moody, 1968.

Hofstadter, R. and Metzger, W. P. *The Development of Academic Freedom in the United States*. New York: Columbia Univ. Press, 1955.

Hooykaas, R. *Christian Faith and the Freedom of Science*. London: Tyndale, 1957.

Kirk, Russell. *Academic Freedom*. Chicago: Regnery, 1955.

Miller, Alexander S. *Faith and Learning: Christian Faith and Higher Education in Twentieth-Century America*. New York: Association, 1960.

Nash, Arnold S. *The University and the Modern World: An Essay in the Philosophy of University Education*. New York: Macmillan, 1944.

Pattillo, M. M. and MacKenzie, D. M. *Church-Sponsored Higher Education in the United States*. Washington, D.C.: American Council on Education, 1966.

Schmidt, G. P. *The Liberal Arts College*. New Brunswick, N.J.: Rutgers Univ. Press, 1957.

St. Olaf College Self-Study Committee. *Integration in the Christian Liberal Arts College*. Northfield, Minn.: St. Olaf College Press, 1956.

Tewksbury, D. G. *The Founding of American Colleges and Universities Before the Civil War*. Hamden, Conn.: Archon Books, 1965 (1st publ., 1932).

Trueblood, Elton. *The Idea of a College*. New York: Harper, 1959.

Von Grueningen, J. P. (ed.). *Toward a Christian Philosophy of Higher Education*. Philadelphia: Westminster, 1957.

Wicke, Myron F. *The Church-Related College*. Washington, D.C.: The Center for Applied Research in Education, Inc., 1964.

Zylstra, Henry. *Testament of Vision*. Grand Rapids, Mich.: Eerdmans, 1961.